Grace
and
Humanness

Grace
and
Humanness

Theological Reflections Because of Culture

Orlando O. Espín

ORBIS BOOKS

Maryknoll, New York 10545

Founded in 1970, Orbis Books endeavors to publish works that enlighten the mind, nourish the spirit, and challenge the conscience. The publishing arm of the Maryknoll Fathers and Brothers, Orbis seeks to explore the global dimensions of the Christian faith and mission, to invite dialogue with diverse cultures and religious traditions, and to serve the cause of reconciliation and peace. The books published reflect the views of their authors and do not represent the official position of the Maryknoll Society. To learn more about Maryknoll and Orbis Books, please visit our website at www.maryknoll.org.

Manufactured in the United States of America.

Library of Congress Cataloguing-in-Publication Data

Espín, Orlando.
  Grace and humanness : theological reflections because of culture / Orlando O. Espín.
     p. cm.
   ISBN 978-1-57075-730-3
1. Christianity and culture. 2. Theological anthropology. I. Title.
   BR115.C8E76 2007
   261--dc22
                              2007005784

Para Ricardo, compañero y amigo.

Para Estela, Laura, Rodolfo, Ramiro, Ana Laura,
Fernanda y Karolina.

Y para Carolina.

*No va para ningún lado
quien no sabe dónde está.*
Gilberto Santa Rosa

Contents

Introduction

In 1996 a number of friends and colleagues encouraged me to select a few of my previously published articles and gather them into a single volume. The common thread of those articles was popular Catholicism, and the result was *The Faith of the People: Theological Reflections on Popular Catholicism* (Maryknoll, N.Y.: Orbis Books, 1997). I must admit that I was surprised at how well received the book was, and am grateful to many readers for their comments.

Ten years later, in 2006, friends and colleagues have again encouraged me to select and bring into one book other texts. The result of this new selection is the present volume. It is not a continuation of *The Faith of the People*, despite some similarities.

The present collection still reflects on popular Catholicism— the theological study of which has been the main focus of my professional life. It also takes a theological look at another popular religion—more specifically, the Lukumí religion, which is present in many U.S. Latino/a communities. But what is more important, this new volume brings up issues that culture raises for theology.

A very evident thread tying together all chapters of this book is my ongoing reflection on culture. Whether it is culture as the inevitable context of all theologizing, interculturality as theological method in our globalized and globalizing world, or the contributions of/from Latino/a cultures to theology, the common thread is clear and (I hope) my arguments and conclusions are too.[1]

Is there a theology that is not contextual? Has there ever been a theologian who is not contextualized? All theologies and all theologians are culturally bound, and there can be no exception. All theologies and all theologians, therefore, are inescapably limited and particular in their respective methods, perspectives, and assumptions. The so-called theological mainstream, therefore, seems as particular and limited as the minorities that jointly are (and have always been) the majority. With many others, I have often said that power asymmetries and the exercise of dominant power arguably are, to this day, the main underlying explanations for mainstream theologians' and theologies' assumed pretensions to universality or to universal validity—pretensions all too often accompanied by the de facto disregard of theologies that do not display or acknowledge the "approval" and logic of the dominant in academy, church, and society. This book wants to again make the point and (in various ways) justify it.

"Grace and Humanness" was the title of a paper I presented over a decade ago at an ecumenical gathering of Latino/a theologians in Atlanta.[2] I have adopted it for the present volume because I believe that all that Christian theologies could ever say about gospel, faith, and the Christian life can be ultimately boiled down to grace *and* humanness. As I argued in the paper whose name this book now bears, the experience of grace is always and inevitably cultural, and our cultural humanness is indeed graced. Borrowing the title of that paper, therefore, seemed apt for this book.

One last point. On the dedicatory page I have included a phrase from the lyrics of a salsa by Puerto Rican singer and composer Gilberto Santa Rosa. *No va para ningún lado quien no sabe dónde está* ("you won't go anywhere unless you first know where you are at") is a good way of summarizing the main point of this volume.

Most of the texts in this new collection have never been published but were presented as papers at national or foreign theological meetings. At the beginning of each chapter a note indicates its provenance.

I want to thank Prof. Carmen M. Nanko-Fernández (Catholic Theological Union, Chicago), Prof. Jean-Pierre Ruiz (St. John's University, New York), Prof. Miguel Díaz (St. John's University, Collegeville), Prof. Michelle González (University of Miami), and Prof. Bernard Cooke (San Diego State University) for their many suggestions and frequent encouragement.

I especially need to thank Prof. Patricia Plovanich, Prof. Gary Macy, and Prof. Russell Fuller (my colleagues at the University of San Diego) for their constant support, their impressive theological, biblical, and historical expertise, and their healthy critique. Frequent conversations with them have led to my clarifying and fine-tuning the reflections on many of the issues raised in the present volume. Theologians occasionally admit how much their friendships with colleagues impact and shape their thought. I readily admit it here, and express my gratitude to them.

The aforementioned colleagues and friends, and also those who regularly participate in the colloquia of the Academy of Catholic Hispanic Theologians of the United States (ACHTUS) and in the work of the Black Catholic Theological Symposium (BCTS) have, through their shared reflections, significantly contributed to mine over the past many years.

Finally, I cannot end this introduction without thanking Robert Ellsberg and the staff at Orbis Books. Their unswerving support for Latino/a theology is real. They too made this volume possible.

Fall 2006
University of San Diego

Notes

1. I had some difficulty in deciding which texts to include. Colleagues made some suggestions. Without going far from the study of popular Catholicism, I wanted to focus on culture, and this has been the main criterion of selection. Given the nature of any collection of texts originally written in and for different contexts, the reader will herein find some inevitable (and, I hope, not annoying) repetitions.

2. The papers presented at the Atlanta meeting were published in *We Are a People! Initiatives in Hispanic American Theology,* ed. R. S. Goizueta (Minneapolis, Minn.: Fortress Press, 1992). Miguel Díaz extensively discussed my paper, from the perspective of theological anthropology, in his *On Being Human: U.S. Hispanic and Rahnerian Perspectives* (Maryknoll, N.Y.: Orbis Books, 2001).

1

Toward the Construction
of an Intercultural Theology
of (Catholic) Tradition

Introduction

In contemporary European and North American Catholic scholarship, there has been a growing interest in the theology of tradition. Recent works by Robert Schreiter, Terrence Tilley, John Thiel, Siegfried Wiedenhofer, Richard Gaillardetz, M. Shawn Copeland, and others indicate the interest that various theories of tradition can raise among theologians.[1] These and other Catholics are joined by Protestant scholars, and by academics in philosophy and the social sciences,[2] thereby giving the study of tradition an increased impetus and a growing contemporary body of literature.

Parallel to this contemporary interest in tradition there has been an equally important growth in the theological study of what has come to be known as "popular Catholicism."[3] U.S. Latino/a theologians have been, for several decades now, at the forefront of this research. The works of Roberto Goizueta, Alejandro García-Rivera, Miguel Díaz, and my own,[4] among many others, are joined

The earliest version of this text was presented as a paper at the 2001 annual convention of the Catholic Theological Society of America, in Milwaukee. A second and longer version appeared in the *Journal of Hispanic/Latino Theology* 9, no. 3 (2002): 22-59. The third and final version (which appears here) was published in *Tradition and Tradition Theories,* ed. T. Larbig and S. Wiedenhofer (Berlin: Lit Verlag, 2006), 281-319.

to publications by Diego Irarrázaval, Manuel Marzal, Christián Parker, William Christian, and others across a number of disciplines on both sides of the Atlantic.[5] Latin American, Asian, and African scholars have become increasingly active and important partners in the interdisciplinary and international dialogue on popular Catholicism *and* on the theology of tradition.[6] And yet, there seems to be little sustained, critical, and theoretical dialogue between those who study tradition and those who study popular Catholicism.

This paper is, first, an attempt at an intercultural approach to the theology of Catholic tradition (and, therefore, *not* an attempt at constructing an overall philosophical or general theory of tradition, although a theologian cannot avoid conversation with philosophers and social scientists on this issue). Second, this paper is an attempt at bringing an intercultural approach to the theology of Catholic tradition into dialogue with a theology of popular Catholicism.[7] This paper is still a work in progress; in significant ways it is a moment in a longer experiment.[8]

But before I go any further let me, as a preliminary statement and in an acknowledgedly incomplete and revisable way, indicate what I mean by the term "tradition," as in the expression "Catholic tradition" (I am intentionally waiting until the end of this paper to offer a more complete and revised understanding of the term). I will then proceed to make some observations on frequent contemporary (theological) approaches to tradition. The constructive part of this paper begins with a brief review of globalization (given that globalization is fast becoming today's context for theologizing), followed by a summary of present-day intercultural thought. I will finally proceed to suggest the reasons for constructing an intercultural theology of tradition (referring back to my first preliminary statement on tradition) and the general contours of that theology.

All religions known to humankind are traditional, in the sense that all religions exist only in time and are, necessarily, situated in history and are heirs of history (whether they perceive/explain themselves historically or not).[9] Religions survive and prolong their existence in time *because* they have managed to create the means of transmitting their beliefs, holy stories, rituals, etc., from one generation to the next. Human beings too are necessarily traditional (in the sense meant here) and cannot be otherwise.[10] From preceding generations, and by varied means of transmission, human beings are "entrusted" with language, customs, values, thought patterns, etc.; and while "in their trust," these elements are further shaped, reinterpreted, and made to grow. It is no exaggeration to say that human beings receive their self-understanding, and the tools for it, through and from tradition, just as they in turn reinvent it.

Catholicism can be understood as the organization of a specific collective (and *always present*) Christian interpretation of life's past, present, and future, which in turn creates and sustains the complex mechanism of recall, assumptions, and associations of past events, specific interpretations, and meanings that are distinct to this religion.[11] This collective interpretation (and the mechanism it creates and sustains) is Catholic tradition. Doctrines function within this tradition as reputable indicators of continuity (as continuity is perceived) and, especially, as both frameworks for believers' corporate identity[12] and criteria for correct belief (as every generation attempts to construct, in its present, that corporate identity for itself in continuity with preceding generations of believers). *Tradition, therefore, is not merely or mainly a recall of the past or a reference to it. Rather, it is the present interpretation of the past in reference to the future.* Present interests and hopes for the future drive and legitimize the complex web of recalls, assumptions, and associations we call the past. Thus, the present projects a future that needs to be legitimized by a past that is, or so it seems, constructed by interpretations of and from the present's memory; and, in doing this, the present "creates" a past that is then declared to be *the* stable, self-evident, and "objectively there" past, ready to be mined for justifications for the present's needs of legitimation. I do not need to add that the past did exist (and I am not claiming otherwise), but our reception of that past, our interpretations of it, and our varied configurations of it are all present constructs.

In this case, is there such a thing as "continuity" in the tradition? I believe there is, and for several reasons. Catholic tradition is collective, and, consequently, it is *the whole people* who must attest to a new interpretation's coherence or coincidence with earlier ones. But because a whole people may sense coherence or coincidence with its recalled past (or with this past's understandings), it does not necessarily imply or mean that the sensed present coherence or coincidence is anything but an interpretation of what may or may not have actually been. Continuity in tradition exists, therefore, *if and when the people believe that continuity exists.* Continuity, furthermore, is the attempt by every present generation of Catholics to legitimize its corporate identity by recalling (in the present) those associations, assumptions, and interpretations from the past that contribute to what (in the present) is held to guarantee the continuity of the present generation's claimed Catholic identity. Continuity, also, is an affirmation of life—not in the sense of individualistic life, but life as life-in-community. It is to affirm the whole church as the preeminent subject of tradition.

There is, however, an indispensable criterion which is the gauge by which doctrines or practices are most frequently judged by the people to be in continuity with Catholic identity and tradition: namely, *whether or not a doctrine or practice is in coherence and/or coincidence with the people's own present religion.* I am in no way implying or suggesting that the people's Catholicism is *the* criterion (or the best or most important criterion). I am very much saying, however, that the ordinary way of judging the legitimacy of any claim to continuity (i.e., of judging what presents itself, in doctrine or practice, as a legitimate and necessary element of Catholic tradition, and thus constitutive of Catholic identity) is popular Catholicism.[13] The everyday faith and faith-life of everyday Catholics is the ordinary means by which Catholic tradition is interpreted and constructed, Catholic identity shaped, and continuity with the past claimed. This ordinary, collective interpretation *is* Catholic tradition. Popular Catholicism acts as both framework for the people's corporate Catholic identity and as the criterion for correct belief and behavior (as every generation of Catholics attempts to construct that identity for itself in continuity with preceding generations of Catholics). Development or change in the tradition, consequently, seems to occur ordinarily within the mesh and fabric of popular Catholicism.

Some Observations on Recent Theologies of Tradition vis-à-vis the Contemporary World

I said earlier that intercultural approaches seemed, in my estimation, to be very important for an adequate theology of tradition today. We live in a world context that is increasingly and irreversibly globalized. This is important not only for those who study economic and market theory and systems. An understanding of globalization is absolutely crucial for any contemporary theology that attempts to speak as *catholic* (with both lower case and upper case "C").

One of the great tensions in today's world is between particularities and universalities, and the claims made by all. These tensions will display themselves, and demand reflection, in any theology of tradition today.

Particularity does not cancel but is rather the condition for universality. The particularly cultural and the culturally particular are conditions for intercultural, global dialogue. To speak of tradition today is to speak not just in the universal church, but to speak in the globalized and globalizing world—with all this implies—from within the cultural universes of a myriad particularities. Intercultural thought, it seems to me, has developed as a potentially important means for establishing a theological dialogue on tradition that is not naive vis-à-vis the realities of globalization, and which is also respectful of the particularities of human communities and cultures.

Christianity exists only in the world. In *this* world, as *this* world is. This is evident. And just as evident is the mutually impacting relationship between Christianity and the worlds in which it exists and has existed. The various shapes of this mutually impacting relationship are and have been very diverse, but the fact remains: Christianity exists only in this world, and it impacts it as much as this world impacts Christianity.

Today's Christianity exists in an increasingly and irreversibly globalizing world, and yet this same world seems equally and increasingly emphatic about its ethnic and cultural diversity. It might seem, at first glance, that these two facets of our contemporary world are contradictory, although a deeper analysis suggests that increased globalization and increased diversity are but two faces of the same complex of economic, social, political, and cultural forces at work today. The world in which Christianity now finds itself is increasingly "one" and increasingly "catholic" (i.e., globalized and diverse). It would be a mistake to choose one facet of today's world over the other (e.g., globalization over diversity, or vice versa) as the best category of analysis of contemporary reality. It would also be a grave theoretical error to limit the interpretation and analysis of today's world to the perspectives or interests of either those who benefit from globalization or those whom globalization leaves behind.

And yet, theologians of tradition have too frequently limited themselves to interpretive analyses and categories that were born in and for what we often call the First World—or said in other words, analyses and categories of the theological study of tradition usually come from the perspective of the beneficiaries of globalization.[14] As a consequence, the intellectual, social, and other interests of the First World permeate and blindfold many recent Catholic theologies of tradition. Judging from the philosophical thought, historical studies, and social-scientific works that most theologians appeal to when working on tradition, one would think that European and European American constructs are sufficient for the development of Catholic theologies of tradition.

It is theologically problematic to see Catholic theologies of tradition ignore the philosophical, historical, and social-scientific contributions of Latin America, Africa, and Asia, as well as the contributions of non-European cultural communities in both Europe and North America.[15] In other words, it is theologically problematic to see Catholic theologies of tradition systematically ignore Catholic tradition as the latter is received and lived among the vast majority of Catholics, simply because these are not perceived as part of the First World. One may legitimately wonder how catholic are these Catholic theologies, and how representative and aware they are of Catholicism as it exists in today's world. Obviously, there is no justification whatsoever for this theological provincialism, which, for the majority of Catholics throughout the world, still bears the stench of colonialism. Many recent Catholic theologies of tradition from Europe and North America that sincerely present themselves as legitimately Catholic would be considered irrelevant, colonial, or tainted by most Catholics in today's world, and, in some cases, would be regarded as naive ideological legitimations of First-World interests.

Most theologians are aware of the social, political, gender, cultural, and economic locations and "usages" of their theologies. In theory most of us would agree that Catholic tradition is impacted by the world in which it exists, and this tradition impacts the world as well. But how we understand, define, and analyze this world is extremely important. Indeed, this is not an irrelevant or merely contextual exercise in which theologians must occasionally engage. This "world-locating" and "world-interpreting" analysis can shape and mold our understanding of tradition, or it can blindfold us to other elements that could profoundly critique our constructs.[16]

Contemporary theology, regardless of geographical location, must today construct its understandings of tradition from an analysis of globalization and diversity, because both globalization and diversity are key facets of today's world.[17] Indeed, globalization and diversity are shaping the world within which the theologian exists as a thinking, believing, and living human being (whether the theologian is aware of it or not), molding his/her perceptions and interpretations of daily reality, as well as his/her daily interactions with his/her social, political, cultural, and economic locations. We cannot escape the mutually impacting relationship that exists between contemporary Christian theology (and theologians) and the contemporary world. It is no longer "theology as usual," because the "usual" (from the world's perspective) is no more. This, evidently, applies to theologies of tradition too.

Globalization as the Contemporary Context of Tradition

We live today in an increasingly and irreversibly globalizing and globalized world. We do not have the time here for an exhaustive analysis of globalization and its worldwide effects, or for a thorough presentation of most current studies on globalization. Therefore, let me summarize, in a few synthetic paragraphs, what I think globalization is, does, and tends to, and make a few suggestions as to what globalization might have to do with crafting contemporary theologies of tradition.[18]

By "globalization" is meant here the theoretical paradigm that attempts to describe humanity's current stage, with special emphasis on the development of worldwide capitalism, as *the* new cultural context. There is no commonly agreed definition of globalization, but most scholars indicate that globalization at least refers to "the increasingly interconnected character of the political, economic, and social life of the peoples on this planet."[19] Globalization became evident after the 1970s, first in the economic arena, with the growth of truly transnational corporations. More concretely, globalization has become the extension of the effects of modernity and postmodernity to the entire world, accompanied by the compression of time and space brought about by communication technologies.

Has globalization brought benefits? The answer clearly depends on the answerer's location. For most of us across the First World (and among some groups in the rest of the world), the advances in technology and science are beneficial. And so are many of the global emphases on human rights, on democratization, on expansion of public education, and the measurable increase in overall quality of life and financial security. I am the first one to admit that as an academic, working in a First-World university, and participating in a First-World society, globalization has benefited me and my family.[20] I suspect that most First-World theologians can say the same. It would be morally dishonest, however, if we placed ourselves and the benefits we have received as the criterion by which to judge globalization. Globalization's benefits to us, and to many like us, have come with the price tag of the increased impoverishment and marginalization of millions of human beings (many of whom are our fellow Catholics) across most of the world. Globalization's beneficial byproducts have come at a high and morally unacceptable human cost. And theologians, consequently, have to be very careful in their choice of philosophical, social-scientific, and economic dialogue partners, because we could naively be contributing (and probably are contributing) the ideological legitimation for the misery of millions of human beings (even if only by simply incorporating the theoretical, philosophical constructs of the First-World academy without a rigorous ethical analysis of their implications and consequences for the rest of the planet).[21]

For us in the First World, and for some groups across the Third, globalization can be easily identified or confused with our societies' progress and technological advances. In other words, because we are the beneficiaries of globalization, we can fall into the trap of thinking that our perceptions and analyses of globalization, and the analytic tools we have developed within and for our First-World contexts, are sufficient and adequate in order to understand globalization. But globalization is global, and this means that the other two-thirds of the planet are impacted by globalization too, but not in the frequently beneficial manner experienced by and in the First World.[22] To understand globalization adequately, therefore, we need to incorporate into our analysis the experiences and data on globalization in and from the Third World, and certainly not through the unquestioned application of analytic tools developed for and within the First World, but precisely through an intercultural dialogue that must engage the application of theoretical tools developed for and within the Third World. We in the First World are not the only ones with rigorous and serious analyses of globalization, its premises and its consequences, although the forces dominant in globalization have very successfully tried to silence most alternative views by making us academics in the First World consider the alternatives as marginally interesting, insufficiently rigorous, or applicable only among the peoples whence these analyses come. When we study globalization from a more comprehensive, global perspective, what else do we find?

Globalization has brought a real decrease in the functions and power of nations and of national governments. The globalized economy has become "de-territorialized."[23] Access to cultural and symbolic goods is now increasingly de-territorialized through de-territorialized means, as is the case with the Internet and other "virtual" vehicles. Divisions among human groups are increasingly dependent on access to the Internet and other similar means, and much less dependent on territories of residence, national citizenship, and so on.

Contemporary capitalism has become global, thereby surpassing the strictly national, international, or multinational. Territorial states (i.e., nations) no longer set enforceable limits or standards of production. Territorial states no longer have the determining power to control transnational corporations. If attempts are made by national governments to control standards or legal arrangements, the transnational corporations simply move somewhere else, thereby making governmental attempts at control increasingly meaningless. The transnational corporations are no longer tied to a territory, a culture, or a nation. The consequences of this new reality are enormous for the national states, the labor market, the very concept of nation, and human cultures.[24]

The globalization of the economy is becoming the foundation of very profound cultural changes across the world, because corporate profits today depend in a very significant way on the transnational corporations' ability to globally "place" their products, with the greatest speed and efficiency possible. It seems evident that profits today depend less on the manufacture of products and more on the efficient, fast, and successful distribution of these products. The consequences of this new situation for workers across the world also seem evident: labor is increasingly globalized, with transnational corporations going wherever they find better labor conditions, fewer restrictions, and greater possibilities for the successful distribution of their products. Therefore, national labor codes, created for the protection of workers, can actually lead to unemployment and "unprotection" of the very workers the labor codes wanted to protect. On the other hand, for the transnational corporations the ideal labor force is the one less protected but better trained in the contemporary, global means of production and distribution. The poor, on both counts, are left behind.

In the process of the de-territorialization of capital, what becomes globalized are not only economic strategies and institutions; ideas, thought processes, and sociocultural patterns of behavior are also globalized and de-territorialized. Breaking cultural, social, political, and ideological barriers (which had been built over the centuries), the mass media and other means of massive and instant communication have shaped, and continue to shape, a truly global mass culture. A whole universe of symbols and signs is now broadcast and distributed globally by the modern means of communications, thereby defining anew the manner in which millions of persons throughout the world think, feel, desire, imagine, and act. Signs and symbols are increasingly disconnected from historical, religious, ethnic, national, or linguistic particularities, becoming de-territorialized and global.

There is little doubt that globalization has appropriated those elements of modernity and postmodernity that serve its de-territorializing, global project, although globalization should not be simply confused with the human historical stages usually referred to as modernity and postmodernity.[25] Thus, for example, globalization emphasizes the very postmodern attitude that relativizes all claims to truth or to universal validity in order to bring down the cultural, political, or religious barriers that may stand in the way of the methods and activities of the transnational corporations. But at the same time, globalization emphasizes the very modern and universalizing scientific and technological claims made by Western societies since the eighteenth century in their quest to control knowledge and the creation of knowledge in the world, thereby denying scientific and technological legitimacy or equality to any scientific or technological alternative from outside the Western world.

The evident success of the transnational, globalization model in some corners of the world has made the rest of the world (i.e., the vast majority of humans, who are deemed to be "not successful" by the standards of globalization) wish for the success they see elsewhere. Globalization, therefore, is a major force behind, and cause of, migration and immigration.[26]

It would be utterly naive to think that the de-territorialization of the economy, of cultural imagination, and even of human identities somehow follows or obeys the dynamics of equality or democracy. In fact, globalization seems to imply and assume the construction of new hierarchies of power, of new power structures across the world. What globalization brings is a new, asymmetric distribution of privileges and exclusions, of possibilities and of hopelessness, of freedoms and slaveries.[27] During the last three millennia, asymmetric power relations in the world were organized so that the rich needed the poor (whether it was for the rich to "save their souls" through works of charity on behalf of the poor, or to exploit the poor through labor in order to increase the rich's wealth). Now, in these globalized times, the poor seem to be increasingly unnecessary. Wealth and capital grow without the work of the poor because, among other reasons, the labor force needed in the globalized economy is a smaller and trained labor force which, almost by definition, prevents the participation of the poor. Globalization is a new way of producing wealth, but it is also, and concomitantly, a new way of producing poverty.

Globalization is not something that occurs outside of us, somehow alienating us from a supposedly "true" religious, cultural, national, or personal "essence." Globalization occurs within and among all of us, and beyond us. And in this sense one could say that globalization is always experienced "locally."[28] Globalization has impacted and continues to impact cultures, belief systems, and epistemologies: our ways of being, of thinking, of knowing, of acting, and of believing.[29]

Globalization presents and understands itself to be *the* viable model for humanity's present and future. This implies that, from globalization's perspective, no other model can been judged to be a viable alternative—not within the First World, and not anywhere else. Globalization, therefore, includes forces of homogenization, of worldwide standardization at every level (cultural, social, political, economic, religious), and thus globalization is inimical to true diversity and to respectful, meaningful dialogue. In other words, globalization represents the new imperial quest and legitimizing ideology of the dominant economic and political forces of today's world, which are no longer territorial states, as in the past, but transnational corporations and interests. And just as in the past, imperial quests mandate conquest and colonization of the weak for the benefit of the strong because, in the logic of globalization, the weak (or those perceived as weak by the dominant) have no viable right or possibility to determine their lives, to choose which economic configuration their societies should adopt, or to maintain and develop their cultural uniqueness.

The forces dominant in globalization have been busy at promoting scholarship that would substantiate the "inevitability" of globalization and the "goodness" of its paradigm for humanity's future. Within the logic of globalization, all stress on the uniqueness or diversity of specific human groups is either coopted as a step toward de-territorialization, or castigated and decried as an illusion that brings division and tension to the global village.

What does globalization have to do with the theology of tradition? To answer, I would first point to the unavoidable ethical dimension and demands placed on all theology that claims to be Christian and on the theologians who craft it. I would also propose that all contemporary theologies of tradition should pay close attention to the location whence they come.

In other words, any theology of tradition today cannot avoid the challenges of and the questions raised by globalization and, more specifically, any theology of tradition cannot avoid the ethical and epistemological questions raised by the choices made when selecting analytic tools and dialogue partners. Whose understanding and experience of tradition is being presented as tradition or as theology of tradition? Whose world, whose social class, whose gender, whose race, whose ethnic and cultural contexts are assumed as typical of, or a standard among, Catholics worldwide?

I have no doubt that all theologians, myself included, inescapably reflect their own location in their theological constructs. I am suggesting here, however, that we in the First World cannot uncritically assume our location to be typical of Catholicism, especially when dealing with a subject like tradition, which evidently involves the identity and faith of the worldwide Catholic community, two-thirds of whose members are in the Third World and are not the beneficiaries of globalization, and who consequently can and do experience tradition, and Catholic identity and faith, in ways significantly different from Catholics in the First World.[30]

Some contemporary Catholic (American) theologies of tradition, tend to display a certain First-World provincialism which might be understandable and perhaps forgiven, if it weren't for the fact that, being scholarly constructs of the First World, these theologies blindfold First-World Catholic scholars and Catholic people to the faith and experience of two-thirds of the church, and further contribute to the silencing in the First World as well as in the Third of viable alternatives and analyses offered by non–First-World Catholic reflections on tradition. And, just as I suggested earlier that the way to a comprehensive and global understanding of globalization required serious intercultural dialogue, so here I again suggest that the way to a comprehensive and truly catholic understanding of Catholic tradition requires serious intercultural dialogue. But what is this intercultural dialogue?

Intercultural Thought and Dialogue

The theories that today we may gather under the rubric "intercultural thought," with a number of allied fields, seem to have coalesced in the late 1980s and early 1990s.[31] Scholars, mostly philosophers, from Europe, India, and Latin America have been at the forefront of this movement.

I have found the work of intercultural philosopher Raúl Fornet-Betancourt to be particularly insightful and rich as a dialogue partner for Catholic theology.[32] I will be using Fornet-Betancourt's contributions in what follows, although I cannot and do not make him responsible for my synthesis of his thought or for my use of it.

First of all, we must understand that interculturality is not inculturation.[33] The latter supposes a "canonical something" that exists independent of a culture and that can be "poured" or "transmitted" into other cultures. The canonical something supposed by inculturation assumes, furthermore, an interpretation or understanding possible only within, and from within, a dominant culture, because the canonical something does not interpret itself, and, therefore, does not understand or proclaim itself (or by itself) as canonical. For something in inculturation to be considered canonical implies that someone, in and from a specific cultural horizon, determined (and thus, because of a set of interests proper to the cultural horizon of the one doing the determining) that this something exists and that it is definitively canonical. Inculturation, consequently, includes the possibility, and perhaps the reality, of colonization. Inculturation thus understood[34] has little to do with the truth that is discovered and that convinces, but rather it has to do with the acceptance of someone else's proclamation, inevitably constructed from within the proclaimer's cultural perspective, that the truth being brought to me should or must convince me.

Instead of inculturation we should speak perhaps of "inter-transculturation," whereby another witnesses to me in an open inter-discursive dialogue what he/she understands and lives as truth; and I, within and from within my own cultural perspective, will contrast and perhaps assume that truth, because I have discovered it as truth within and from within my cultural horizon. And I in turn, upon my discovery of truth (possible within and from within my cultural perspective), witness to the other, again in an open inter-discursive dialogue, what I have come to understand and live as truth, inviting the other to question and/or grow in what he/she understands and lives as truth, thereby moving the process into an ever-deepening and continuing dialogue where truth is discovered and affirmed, over and over, through mutual witnessing, contrasting dialogue, and noncolonizing reflection.

The discovery of truth, then, results from intercultural dialogue and contrast and not from arguments and concepts born within a cultural horizon foreign to me and designed to convince me by pulling me away from my own cultural horizon.[35] The argument that truth, including the gospel's truth, must critique cultures cannot be made to imply or provoke colonization, and such would be the implication if the understanding of truth, including the gospel's truth, which is offered for acceptance by another proceeds from a dominant culture or a hegemonic group within a dominant culture that has access to my culture precisely because of their hegemony or dominance, or when the critique of culture is not the historically possible fruit of the receiving culture's own possibilities.

Convivir, which in Spanish means "to live-with," and which is exactly the same as the Latin *convivire*, is the necessary assumption or precondition for interculturality. "To live-with" implies, among other things, that those who *conviven* are actually present with and to one another for a sufficiently prolonged period of time and, further, that their presence with and to one another engages them with and in one another's daily lives in ways that *each* considers sufficiently meaningful and sufficiently mutually respectful.[36]

Truth is a cultural and an intercultural process. No culture, and no cultural situation, may be considered as the definitive locus of truth or as the best vehicle for the expression of truth.[37] Cultures offer us only the possibilities and instruments for seeking after truth. Truth will only unveil itself to us if we are willing (in intercultural dialogue) to risk contrasting *our* truth with the truth claims and/or truth expressions originating in other cultures. Reality, and thus truth, is not monochrome or monovalent; rather, reality, and thus truth, is plurichrome and plurivalent. There are many versions of reality and, consequently, many versions of truth.

It would be dangerous nonsense to assume in today's globalized and globalizing world that the truth claims of one religious or national group are universally valid just because this one group has, through its own cultural categories and assessment, discovered or affirmed something to be true. By "universal validity" I mean that a truth claim, from within a specific culture, is presented to and is possibly imposed on the potential recipients because the claim's birthing culture assumes its particular perspectives (i.e., its questions and themes, its answers and solutions, its practices and approaches) to be applicable to and correct for all other cultures. The claim to universal validity has usually accompanied the history of power and colonization and has been all too frequently legitimized by these. Unless a group acknowledges to itself and others that there are indeed other claims to truth, just as evidently true within and through other equally legitimate cultural categories, the group's claims to universal validity may be regarded either as an indication of human hubris or as a violation of other people's right to cultural self-determination.[38]

Only in intercultural dialogue, contrasting truth claims with one another, can there begin to appear what may be said to be a universally relevant truth claim. By "universal relevance" I mean that a truth claim may be offered from within a specific culture or group to others who may find the claim to be useful, suggestive, or even true, thereby opening for and within the recipients perspectives (e.g., questions and themes, answers and solutions, practices and approaches, etc.) that had hitherto remained closed, confused, or ignored. It might be possible to discover common threads and denominators among the truth claims with universal relevance, but the original claim does not present itself as necessarily applicable or correct for all possible recipients and in all possible cultural contexts. The recipients must consent to the relevance of the claim that is offered to them. Only in the contrasting intercultural dialogue necessary for the discovery of universally relevant claims can truth be acknowledged, and only then can truth unveil itself without the trappings of empire, imposition, or idolatry.

I realize that the concern for relativism immediately comes to mind. How do we avoid relativism in such intercultural dialogue? There is no limitless relativism involved in the contrasting intercultural dialogue that leads to universally relevant truth claims because, first, there is no limitless number of cultures or of cultural contexts or of truth claims. Second, the fear of relativism is itself a culturally grounded and culturally legitimized fear;[39] and a history of the cultural fear of relativism might unveil it as more intimately connected with power structures and concerns than we might care to admit; in other words, the cultural fear of relativism might be discovered to have less to do with truth itself and more to do with some groups' need to make claims of "universal validity," which have historically accompanied the exercise of dominant power.[40] Third, it might be important to pluck our understanding of truth from the prison of concepts, and to seek it instead in "inter-comprehension" with others (i.e., with others' lives, with others' historical realities, and so on).[41] It might be important to let others, and to let truth itself, be un-defined for us within our own cultural perspective, letting their alterity communicate with us as alterity and, therefore, without necessarily cleanly fitting within our categories. This "in-definition" has nothing to do with relativism; on the contrary, it is the humble acceptance of our own cultural limitation and a critique of our own cultural inclination to intellectual self-idolatry.

Truth, because it exists only culturally for humankind, is and must always be polyphonic. The music produced by a symphonic orchestra is not the result of a single instrument or of a single musician. The music produced by an orchestra results only when each instrument and each musician plays his/her part, with the tonalities and expertise required for each part; and only when all play together as an ensemble may we then hear the fullness of the symphonic composition played by the orchestra. And yet, no one orchestra can ever claim to have the definitive and exclusive interpretation of a given composition. Indeed, no composition could ever claim to be the definitive musical creation. Does this imply relativism? Not at all, because there is, at any point in history, a limited number of instruments, a limited number of musicians, a limited number of compositions, and a limited number of orchestras, besides a limited number of musical notes and the limited human auditive organ. Therefore, the admission of diversity, of particularities, and of limitation, does not necessarily imply relentless relativism. Rather, what we might culturally fear or label as relativism might in fact be no more than necessary and inevitable pluralism, which is a condition for the possibility of community, and indeed for catholicity itself.

One important intercultural concern is how to integrate the diversity of the world into each cultural particularity (opposed to and different from the attempt to integrate the culturally particular into some sort of evident human universality). The postmodern emphasis on cultural particularity seems to have little future in the world of globalization because cultural particularities, seen from many postmodern perspectives, appear to close themselves off to the world's diversity instead of seeking to integrate diversity into the cultural particularities.[42] Some postmodern perspectives presume that diversities need not dialogue in mutually challenging, critiquing, or enriching ways. Confronted with the contemporary difficulty of making universally valid claims, many postmodern philosophical views on particularities have practically chosen to enclose themselves within their particular cultural worlds, giving up on the need[43] for intercultural dialogue that might unveil universally relevant truth, while philosophically legitimizing this closing-off as the intellectually honest and best option. There sometimes seems to be an implied universally valid truth claim made on behalf of postmodernism's denial of universally valid claims!

First-World postmodernism can become an attempt at ethically justifying self-sufficiency and the silencing of the voices of the others, especially when the others might either challenge our self-sufficiency, our particular cultural hubris, our silence in situations of injustice, or the asymmetric and unfair power structures of globalization, which clearly benefit many of the First-World proponents of postmodernity.[44] Moreover, postmodern proposals are mostly lacking in the analyses of their ethical responsibilities in today's globalized and globalizing world.[45] Many of the postmodern views on particularity can become enclosed circles, which risks ultimate sterility. What is ethically needed is a radical critique of each cultural particularity's self-sufficiency, as well as a radical and critical openness to the others who question and challenge our cultural particularity toward solidarity with them, even, and especially, when there is no benefit to be obtained for our particularity in and through that solidarity.[46] This seems to be the ethical way to avoid drowning in our First-World cultural specificity and avoiding moral deafness at the crucifixion of the majority of humans in the globalized world. Contemporary First-World postmodernism, by arguing that its views are the best philosophical explanations for and in today's globalized world, is but refashioning and preserving the same old and tired First-World colonial mentality which in past centuries set itself up as the world's standard and silenced most alternative voices.[47] The alternative to First-World postmodern approaches is not the return to what has been called foundationalism.[48] The alternative, I suggest, is intercultural dialogue, which can acknowledge and accept much of postmodernism's critique of foundationalism while refusing to share postmodernism's inclination to sterile particularisms or its uncritical and ideological legitimation (by omission) of the First World's interests.

There are no multiple particularities and one evident human universality; rather, there are multiple historical, cultural, human universalities which can encounter one another, which can challenge one another, and which through intercultural dialogue might engage in the process of unveiling universally relevant truth.[49] Each one of the multiple universalities acts as the platform from which a way of thought is opened and launched in the world—opening and launching each universality to dialogue with other universalities and with other truth processes. Our own historical, cultural universality is but the first point of reference from which to know and say what is ours, insofar as it is our concrete life and universe of thought. But it is also our first point of reference in learning and perceiving the contingency of our knowing and saying. This discovery of self-contingency is a sine qua non condition for self-critiquing our historical, cultural universality, thereby avoiding the self-idolatry of our historical, cultural universe. By acknowledging the contingency of our universality, and of its knowing, living, and saying, we open our universality to the possibility, indeed to the need, for dialogue, for learning from other historical and cultural universalities, and for allowing our universality to be called to solidarity with others. Dialogue with others and self-critique are not and cannot merely be options or possibilities, although they most certainly are. Dialogue and self-critique should be recognized as needs of life, without which any cultural, historical universality simply withers into self-idolatry and ultimate meaninglessness.

Consequently, intercultural dialogue is the opposite of the First World's dominant provincialism, whereby the dominant Western cultures decree and define their own universality as the only universally valid universality. Intercultural dialogue does not engage in First-World postmodernism's underlying colonial proposal as the best philosophical standard for the globalized world, even when postmodernism publicly claims the exact opposite.[50]

Intercultural dialogue does not assume or propose any culture, any universality, or any philosophical or theological current as the best way for the world.[51] Indeed, intercultural dialogue assumes itself to be also in need of critique, because it too acknowledges itself as contingent. It holds radically open to correction that the process of contrasting conversation, where all is risked in and for the sake of truth-searching dialogue, is capable of determining or clarifying what intercultural dialogue should be and how it should be carried out. And, as a consequence, only through the contrasting and difficult process of unveiling universally relevant truth will universally relevant truth be unveiled without imposition, without colonization, and with the utmost respect for all who engage in this search.

There is a need in theology, and in philosophy and the social sciences, to multiply and broaden the sources.[52] This does not simply mean that we have to add to the list of sources the names and contributions of other objects of study we might have set aside in the past, although this addition might prove itself important too.[53] By "multiplying and broadening the sources of theology," I mean that the voices of other, previously unheard or silenced theologizing subjects must be heard and considered on an equal basis as the voices of the theologizing subjects of Europe and European America. In other words, the theologizing subjects from nondominant communities must be positively and actively acknowledged as being also at the theological table (at the *con-vivencia*), and as always having been there, even if mostly unheard and disregarded, as bearers of perspectives, alternatives, universalities, logic, and truth, and as theologizing subjects who might challenge and critique that which First-World theology assumed to be self-evident.[54]

Intercultural thought requires that we learn to think in new ways. We need to think in new "con-vocative" and "re-perspectivizing" ways.[55] In other words, interculturality invites us to go beyond attempts at "enriching" our First-World perspectives by somehow incorporating the contributions of others, because this enrichment approach would ultimately leave our assumptions and methods untouched and uncritiqued, since it would be through them that we enrich what already is. The *novum* in the new way of thinking is found in risking our assumptions and methods by contrasting them with the assumptions and methods of others, and through this contrasting dialogue being willing to give up some or many of our assumptions and methods and to acquire new ones in and through the intercultural contrasting dialogue. We are thus called to see ourselves, our cultural universalities, our histories, and our lives, as well as our theological assumptions and methods, in the new light offered us by those who are culturally different from us. Consequently, we re-perspectivize our theology as a result of accepting the "con-vocation" of others (a "con-vocation" that is no more and no less a dialogue of many voices: all equal, all heard, all respected, all critiqued, and all challenged). The new way of intercultural thinking is thus polyphonic, because it would ultimately lead us to see our theology, as well as our cultures and history, as "respective," as definitionally bound and related to and with others, thereby negating the temptation to self-enclosing idolatry and culturally feared relativism.

It should be apparent that any serious intercultural dialogue relies on there being conditions for dialogue.[56] This should be obvious from what I have been discussing above. The conditions for dialogue that I am referring to include the political, economic, social, gender, and other dimensions, that contextualize any intercultural exchange today. Therefore, before any serious conversation can occur, the theologizing subjects must acknowledge and face the issues and consequences provoked by these dimensions among and for the theologizing subjects, as well as the conditions for or against equality which these may imply for intercultural dialogue. Once again, I recall that theology—indeed, all of Christianity—occurs only in this world as this world exists. Today a decontextualized dialogue (or one that does not begin by acknowledging and facing the dimensions which impinge on its credibility as an honest search for truth) would be an ideological exercise that can benefit only those who are favored by globalization.[57]

One last and important note on cultures. All human cultures are primarily the historically and ecologically possible means and ways through which people construct and unveil themselves (to themselves, and secondarily to others) as meaningfully human, constructing the meaning of "human" too in this same process.[58] The values, meanings, and goals of cultures, which define the human communities that construct them, have serious consequences on the social organization of the contextual-material universes that these communities affirm as their own because they are in them. Even the most marginalized cultures are still meaningful vehicles of meaningful interpretations of life and reality for the communities that construct and claim them. And it is within and from within this meaningfulness that human communities create and speak their logic, their perspectives, their sense of life, and engage in the quest for truth. It is within and from within this meaningfulness too that human communities universalize their interpretive universes. True universality, thus, is not the decontextualization of thought or concepts, as globalization and modernity might lead some to believe, but the dialogue that engages the human communities' meaningful vehicles of meaningful interpretations of themselves and their worlds (i.e., their cultures), acknowledging each and every one of them as human and potentially relevant, and thereby suggesting that there is a "human" condition which, although constructed and defined in and by every particular universality, can, by contrasting dialogue, be effectively acknowledged as possessing universally relevant elements or description.[59]

Furthermore, because the intercultural view of culture is historical (in Ignacio Ellacuría's sense of the term),[60] it presupposes that no culture is a monolithic block, as if a culture were the naive or simple development of a single tradition that grew without conflict or contradiction. Rather, every culture bears witness to an internal history of conflict and struggle for the determination and control of its values, meanings, logic, and overall contour. The internal history of struggle for inner cultural hegemony is also part of the global intercultural dialogue, because that internal history remembers other silenced traditions and marginalized life experiences. Each and every human culture could have turned out differently, but if cultures exhibit their current values, meanings, logic, etc., it is because of the struggles for internal hegemony that they historically endured and that resulted in the present outcomes.[61]

This, in turn, leads me to conclude that intercultural dialogue, because it engages human cultures, is not and can never be the goal of theology, but rather a necessary avenue for the joint discovery of viable and universally relevant truth in our globalized and globalizing world. The sacralization of cultures, given every culture's internal history, would itself contradict intercultural dialogue.

Toward the Construction of an Intercultural Theology of Catholic Tradition

Catholic tradition can be understood as the organization of a specific collective (and always present) Christian interpretation of life's past, present, and future, which in turn created and still sustains the complex mechanism of recall, assumptions and associations of past events, specific interpretations and meanings that are distinct to this Catholicism. I said this and what immediately follows at the beginning of this article, and I need to repeat it here again.

Tradition is not merely or mainly the recall of the past or a reference to it. Rather, it is a present interpretation of the past in reference to the future. And, in doing this, the present creates a past that is then declared to be stable, self-evident, "objectively there," and ready to be mined for justifications to the present's legitimation needs. Continuity in tradition exists *if and when the people believe that continuity exists.*

I also said at the beginning that there is an indispensable criterion that is the gauge by which doctrines or practices are most frequently judged by the people to be in continuity with Catholic identity and tradition: namely, whether or not a doctrine or practice is in coherence and/or coincidence with the people's own present religion.

I said at the beginning of this article that this view of tradition is admittedly incomplete and revisable. So let me lay out some first revisions of these incomplete notions. Very simply put, Catholic tradition is the Catholic people's *present* interpretation of the meaning of revelation within and for *present* circumstances, legitimizing this interpretation by appeals to the past, which is understood also as a present interpretation. As interpretation, tradition is a cultural product, but the product of many cultures in many places. Culture is the omnipresent context and means for all present and earlier interpretations of revelation.[62] But cultures bear witness in themselves to their internal history of struggles and conflicts; they are not monochrome, monophonic, or innocent. Consequently, it is not difficult to deduce that Catholic tradition (to the degree that it is a product of culture) also bears the internal mark of struggles and conflicts, and thus tradition is not monochrome, monophonic, or innocent.

As an interpretation constructed by many cultures in many places, Catholic tradition could be understood as the present result of an intercultural web of universalities.[63] This affirms its continuity with an equally plural past, which it chooses to interpret according to the legitimizing needs of the present. It would be clearly naive to assume, however, that all of the cultural universalities that have contributed to Catholic tradition have done so on an equal basis, or that all contributions have been respectfully heard and pondered.[64] There is no point in divorcing the historical development of Catholic tradition from the historical exercise of power by Catholic nations or from the evolution of the exercise of power within Catholicism itself (further understanding that the history of the exercise of economic, political, social, and gender power has benefited some Catholic groups in the church and in the world through alliances with the dominant in First-World cultural contexts).[65] Be that as it may, Catholic tradition is the present, multilayered, and polyphonic construct of many cultural universes attempting to interpret revelation for their diverse presents and from within their diverse cultural perspectives.

Catholic tradition has recognizable unity, but only on the condition that it also be said that Catholic tradition is catholic. Tradition is both one and catholic as long as, by that claim, we do not erase the conditions and demands outlined earlier for intercultural dialogue and for this dialogue's contrasting means of searching for universally relevant truth claims. In other words, the unity and universally relevant truth claims of tradition rest on tradition's inner history of intercultural dialogue.

Why do Catholic tradition's many cultural contributors claim to have arrived, in so many present moments, at what may be a catholic unity of universally relevant truth claims? Walter Kasper has written that apostolic succession in the episcopate can be viewed as the incorporation and reception of new bishops into the apostolic ministry.[66] The public, ecclesial means of this incorporation and reception, of course, have been important; but the point Kasper makes is that the means are not the defining factor of episcopal apostolic succession but incorporation into the apostolic ministry is. This Kasperian insight makes me wonder if it might not be possible to conceive of an intercultural model of tradition that assumes—at any given point in history—a multiplicity of Catholic communities, each with its own understandings and practices, which are "Catholic" according to each community's present and particular criteria, and which are then offered or presented as universally relevant to other Catholic communities worldwide. The communities and their truth claims then become either incorporated or confirmed in worldwide Catholic tradition as they are received and/or recognized by other Catholic communities as bearers of universally relevant truth claims. In this model, Catholic tradition occurs in every Catholic generation and in every Catholic community, as the Catholic communities throughout the world acknowledge one another again and again, in every historical present, as bearers and witnesses of universally relevant truth. This diversity, again according to Kasper, in no way compromises the existence of the universal church but is the possibility for that existence.[67]

This model, which is respectful of the alterity of cultures and assumes a contrasting, dialogical approach, raises questions about the criteria that are needed for assessing the universal relevance, and thus the incorporation and/or confirmation, of the many Catholic particular universes within the Catholic tradition.

In the history of the tradition there seem to be some specific criteria that have been frequently employed to judge the legitimacy of claims to continuity within the tradition, and thus claims of legitimate interpretations of revelation and of universally relevant truth.[68] These criteria gauge the levels of coherence or coincidence of the claims with all, most, or some of the following: (1) the text and message of Scripture; (2) the writings of early Christian authors or doctrines and practices of the early church; (3) the theories and proposals advanced by theologians of past generations; and (4) past statements or doctrinal decisions made by recognized authorities of the church (e.g., ecumenical councils, regional or national synods of bishops, and popes). Written texts have had a primacy in establishing these criteria, but this poses some significant theological difficulties, the least of which is an inadequate understanding and justification of the *sensus fidelium*, as well as of the relation between Scripture and tradition.[69]

There has always been, however, a fifth criterion missing from this list. It is the gauge by which doctrines or practices are and have been most frequently judged to be in continuity with Catholic tradition: *whether a doctrine or practice is in coherence or coincidence with the people's present religion.* The other four criteria, in varying ways and degrees, have entered the judgment of legitimacy occasionally and only as needed: as extraordinary gauges. The everyday faith and faith-life of everyday Catholics have been the ordinary means by which tradition has been, and still is, interpreted and constructed, and Catholic identity shaped.[70]

Catholic doctrine on the *sensus fidelium* intimately connects, I think, with what I have said about popular Catholicism[71] and with Kasper's own insights[72] on the relationship between the universal and the local churches. Popular Catholicism is not monolithic, monochrome, or universally identical. Within it there is immense variety. Catholic communities across the planet, as well as Catholic communities across the centuries, attest to the omnipresence of popular Catholicism, even if the latter's face and contents have changed and continue to change.[73] The people's everyday Catholicism is eminently cultural. In other words, everyday religion is, necessarily and unavoidably, enmeshed in culture. The cultural universes of the Catholic people throughout the world determine the shape and function and, to some degree, the contents of popular Catholicism.

Perhaps our theological reflection on the *sensus fidelium* might admit that the latter exists mainly, if not only, as a Spirit-led process of intercultural contrasting dialogue (on all sorts of faith-related issues) that occurs among and within Catholic communities worldwide, leading (again as a Spirit-led process) toward universally relevant claims that could in time be consensually acknowledged by Catholic communities. With this understanding of the *sensus fidelium*, we can view its contribution to tradition interculturally and appreciate its role as ordinary and as indispensable, because popular Catholicism is, after all, the way most Catholics are Catholic.

To complicate matters, revelation itself, which is interpreted in and by tradition,[74] cannot be divorced from its cultural contexts. Even though I accept and affirm in faith that revelation's ultimate source is God, there is no denying that humans believe in revelation as humans. But to be human has always meant to be necessarily and inevitably located in and contextualized by culture; and in our particular present, to be human necessarily and inevitably localizes and contextualizes us and our reception and interpretations of revelation in our globalizing and globalized world.

An intercultural theology of tradition must squarely face the difficulties implied in relating, on the one hand, intercultural dialogue with its risks and its contrasting approach, and, on the other hand, the myriad particularizing and universalizing cultural horizons of humankind, as a means of constructing a multilayered, polyphonic, and non-innocent model of Catholic tradition. An intercultural theology of tradition, furthermore, must do all of this within the globalized and globalizing world context. And an intercultural theology of tradition should also reflect on the possibilities and contours of intercultural interpretations of revelation, without forgetting to also develop an intercultural definition of revelation.

As an intercultural theology of tradition is constructed (and I am very much aware of the experimental character of the proposal I am making here), this theology must deal with further questions of relativism. I do not think that relentless relativism is the problem; but I imagine that further questions will arise and these will need to be addressed.[75]

There are still other legitimate questions surrounding an intercultural model of tradition that must be addressed—for example, questions that link any model of tradition with Catholic ecclesial realities and ecclesiological doctrines. Among these, I am thinking in particular of the relationship between Scripture and tradition, the relationship between the local churches and the universal church, and the role of the magisterium in discerning claims to continuity and coherence with tradition, and thus in discerning universally relevant truth claims. What role would the papal and episcopal magisterium have, and how would this role be practically constructed, in a model that proposes contrasting intercultural dialogue of all truth claims as the context and vehicle for assessing and acknowledging universally valid claims?[76] How can we interculturally, in a manner that is also theologically acceptable, define revelation, and how precisely can it be interpreted through contrasting intercultural dialogue? The long list of issues is there, and they have to be dealt with in an adequate and coherent way. The ecumenical and interreligious consequences are potentially immense. Nevertheless, I do think that when all is said and the construction done, an intercultural model of tradition will stand up to critique and will show itself a useful and adequate means for understanding Catholic tradition in today's globalized and diverse world.

Finally and most importantly, the construction of an intercultural theology of tradition has to acknowledge that the Spirit of God is at work in this globalized and culturally diverse world of ours. An acknowledgement must lead to an affirmation of the values raised by the Spirit in different Catholic communities across the world and of the Spirit as the ultimate thrust for unity discovered through a contrasting dialogue among the many universally relevant claims made by the communities in the name of the tradition.

The Spirit is at work in and through and in spite of our myriad internal cultural histories of conflict and struggle. Catholic tradition is also the result of the history of grace, because grace,[77] according to Catholic theology, builds on and works through humanness; and humanness is cultural, conflictual, particular, thirsting for transcendence, bound and shaped by the immense complexity of our world. Therefore, tradition is arguably an ever-present context for human encounters with God in and through the immense cultural diversity that the Spirit assumes and fosters. And yet this diversity is no obstacle to the Catholic communities' plural recognition of the Spirit, as Kasper reminds us.[78] In other words, Catholic tradition, because of the action of the Spirit, can be both one and catholic, without in any way disregarding or minimizing one dimension in order to uphold the other; or, said differently, because of the Spirit, tradition can be both global and intercultural.

The unity and diversity of tradition are the work of the Spirit, and although we can and must endeavor to explain through various theological models how this unity and this diversity may be found, the theologian will sooner or later have to admit the mysterious dimension of the work of the Spirit, beyond all the models, all the critiques, and all the explanations. The Spirit, therefore, can keep us from sacralizing any explanatory model, and can thus keep tradition in constant need of interpreting and legitimizing itself as *both* one *and* catholic. It seems to me that in today's world, an intercultural approach offers a very rich and adequate means for understanding Catholic tradition.

Notes

1. As examples, see Robert J. Schreiter, *The New Catholicity: Theology between the Global and the Local* (Maryknoll, N.Y.: Orbis Books, 1997); and idem, "A Semiotic-Linguistic Theory of Tradition: Identity and Communication amid Cultural Difference," in *Zur Logik religiöser Traditionen,* ed. Barbara Schoppelreich and Siegfried Wiedenhofer (Frankfurt a. M.: IKO/Verlag für Interkulturelle Kommunikation, 1998), 87-118; Terrence W. Tilley, *Inventing Catholic Tradition* (Maryknoll, N.Y.: Orbis Books, 2000); John E. Thiel, *Senses of Tradition: Continuity and Development in Catholic Faith* (New York: Oxford University Press, 2000); Siegfried Wiedenhofer, "The Logic of Tradition," in *Zur Logik religiöser Traditionen,* ed. Schoppelreich and Wiedenhofer, 11-84, and idem, "Identität und Kommunikabilität kultureller und religiöser Traditionen im Verständnis christlicher Theologie," in *Zur Logik religiöser Traditionen,* ed. Schoppelreich and Wiedenhofer, 227-63; Richard R. Gaillardetz, "Doctrinal Teaching Authority and the Reception of Doctrine: New Perspectives," in *Authority and Governance in the Church,* ed. Bernard Hoose (London: Ashgate, 2002); M. Shawn Copeland, "Tradition and the Traditions of African American Catholicism," *Theological Studies* 61, no. 4 (2000): 632-55; Catherine Bell, *Who Owns Tradition? Religion and the Messiness of History* (Santa Clara Lectures Series; Santa Clara, Calif.: Santa Clara University/Bannan Institute for Jesuit Education and Christian Values, 2001); David Brown, *Tradition and Imagination: Revelation and Change* (Oxford: Oxford University Press, 1999).

2. See, as examples, Edward Shils, *Tradition* (Chicago: University of Chicago Press, 1981); Jacques LeGoff, *History and Memory* (New York: Columbia University Press, 1992); Stephen H. Watson, *Tradition(s): Refiguring Community and Virtue in Classical German Thought* (Bloomington, Ind.: Indiana University Press, 1997); Paul Heelas, Scott Lash, and Paul Morris, eds., *Detraditionalization: Critical Reflections on Authority and Identity* (Oxford: Blackwell Publishers, 1996); Paul Connerton, *How Societies Remember* (Cambridge: Cambridge University Press, 1989); Danièle Hervieu-Léger, *Religion as a Chain of Memory* (New Brunswick, N.J.: Rutgers University Press, 2000); Joyce Appleby, Lynn Hunt, and Margaret Jacob, *Telling the Truth about History* (New York: W. W. Norton, 1994); Eric Hobsbawm and Terence Ranger, eds., *The Invention of Tradition* (Cambridge: Cambridge University Press, 1987).

3. By "popular" I do not mean "widespread," although popular Catholi-

cism certainly is. The adjective "popular" is related to the noun "people," and thus I use the term to refer to Catholicism as practiced, believed, etc., by the *common* (lay) people *who identify themselves* as part of the Catholic tradition. Some authors have recently suggested that "popular" Catholicism is best referred to as "lived" Catholicism. The proponents' arguments are unconvincing. Is there any type of Catholicism that is not lived? In current U.S. Latino/a scholarship, "popular" remains the more frequent adjective, and for this reason I will continue to use "popular" in this article. In reference to the analytic meaning of "popular," see Geneviève Bollème, *El pueblo por escrito: Significados culturales de lo "popular"* (Mexico City: Fondo de Cultura Económica, 1990).

4. See as examples, Roberto S. Goizueta, *Caminemos con Jesús: Toward a Hispanic/Latino Theology of Accompaniment* (Maryknoll, N.Y.: Orbis Books, 1995); Alejandro García-Rivera, *St. Martin de Porres: The "Little Stories" and the Semiotics of Culture* (Maryknoll, N.Y.: Orbis Books, 1995); and idem, *The Community of the Beautiful: A Theological Aesthetics* (Collegeville, Minn.: Liturgical Press, 1999); Miguel H. Díaz, *On Being Human: U.S. Hispanic and Rahnerian Perspectives* (Maryknoll, N.Y.: Orbis Books, 2001); Orlando O. Espín, *The Faith of the People: Theological Reflections on Popular Catholicism* (Maryknoll, N.Y.: Orbis Books, 1997); and idem with M. H. Díaz, eds., *From the Heart of Our People: Theological Explorations into Catholic Systematic Theology* (Maryknoll, N.Y.: Orbis Books, 1999).

5. See, as examples, Diego Irarrázaval, *Inculturation: New Dawn of the Church in Latin America* (Maryknoll, N.Y.: Orbis Books, 2000); idem, *Teología en la fe del pueblo* (San José, Costa Rica: Editorial DEI, 1999); Manuel Marzal, *El sincretismo iberoamericano* (Lima: Pontificia Universidad Católica del Perú, 1988); Christián Parker, *Otra lógica en América Latina: Religión popular y modernización capitalista* (Santiago de Chile: Fondo de Cultura Económica, 1993); William A. Christian, *Local Religion in Sixteenth-Century Spain* (Princeton, N.J.: Princeton University Press, 1981); and idem, *Moving Crucifixes in Modern Spain* (Princeton, N.J.: Princeton University Press, 1992); Thomas Bamat and Jean-Paul Wiest, eds. *Popular Catholicism in a World Church: Seven Case Studies in Inculturation* (Maryknoll, N.Y.: Orbis Books, 1999); Eamon Duffy, *The Stripping of the Altars: Traditional Religion in England, 1400-1580* (New Haven, Conn.: Yale University Press, 1992); Robert A. Orsi, *Thank You, St. Jude: Women's Devotion to the Patron Saint of Hopeless Causes* (New Haven, Conn.: Yale University Press 1996).

6. An example of this growing international conversation is the important volume coedited by Barbara Schoppelreich and Siegfried Wiedenhofer,

Zur Logik religiöser Traditionen (n. 1, above), as well as the present book and a volume edited by Raúl Fornet-Betancourt, *Kulturen zwischen Tradition und Innovation* (Frankfurt a. M.: IKO/Verlag für Interkulturelle Kommunikation, 2001). The international, intercultural theological and philosophical projects and congresses sponsored by Germany's respected Institute of Missiology (Aachen) have become a further sign of the growing protagonism of Third-World theologians in the study of tradition and popular Catholicism.

7. Later on in this article I will explain the reasons for distinguishing "interculturality" from "inculturation." I also want to clarify here that "interculturality" is not equivalent to "multiculturalism." On the one hand, multiculturalism (as inculturation) often assumes that there is a universally valid "something" that can be communicated or transferred across cultures. Thus, the reasons given below for objecting to inculturation apply, *mutatis mutandi*, to these multicultural approaches. On the other hand, multiculturalism also attempts to bring diverse cultural voices to share in one reality. The difficulties with this approach are grounded on the growing conviction that, culturally speaking, there does not seem ever to be one reality, and further, that the particular reality in which the diverse cultural perspectives are to participate precedes the multicultural and was already established according to and for the benefit of one (dominant) culture's interests. Thus, it is neither innocent nor equally forged by the different participating cultures. On my critique of multiculturalism, see Orlando O. Espín, "A Multicultural Church? Theological Reflections from Below," in *The Multicultural Church: A New Landscape in U.S. Theologies,* ed. William Cenkner (New York: Paulist Press, 1996), 54-71. Some crosscultural approaches seem to be close to what most authors understand as interculturality; but the divergence of views on and within crosscultural studies does not allow for a reasonably conclusive evaluation or synthesis of crosscultural thought at this time.

8. I am finishing a book on the overall topic of the present article. This article's text is a modified and enlarged version of a paper (with similar title) that I presented at the 2001 national convention of the Catholic Theological Society of America, in Milwaukee.

9. See Bell, *Who Owns Tradition?* (n. 1, above).

10. One cannot help recalling Hans-Georg Gadamer's *Wahrheit und Methode* (Tübingen: Mohr/Paul Siebeck, 1975).

11. The several branches of Christianity share much when, in the present, they interpret their common (and partially different) past(s). It might prove ecumenically fruitful for the churches to recognize the inevitable present-day moment and character of their various interpretations of the

Christian past. Perhaps, as suggested by the Rt. Rev. G. Hughes, Episcopal (Anglican) bishop of San Diego, tradition should be understood as a function of the future, in order to construct it today the way we want or need tradition to be tomorrow. Jaroslav Pelikan's *The Vindication of Tradition* (New Haven, Conn.: Yale University Press, 1984), and Justo L. González's *Mañana: Christian Theology from a Hispanic Perspective* (Nashville, Tenn.: Abingdon Press, 1990) are scholarly works that point in the direction suggested by Bishop Hughes. See also the bibliography in the following note.

12. I must add here, because I have just referred to "identity," that it is not understood theologically within Catholicism as being equal to or established by adherence to doctrinal statements or practices of the church's magisterium. Indeed, it would be easy to demonstrate that Catholic identity has been *ordinarily* established or crafted first through (popular) Catholicism's *epistemological lens*. See Espín, *The Faith of the People* (n. 4, above); idem, "An Exploration into the Theology of Grace and Sin," in *From the Heart of Our People,* ed. Espín and Díaz (n. 4, above); idem, "Popular Catholicism as an Epistemology (of Suffering)," *Journal of Hispanic/Latino Theology* 2, no. 2 (1994): 55-78; Alister E. McGrath, *The Genesis of Doctrine: A Study in the Foundation of Doctrinal Criticism* (Oxford: Basil Blackwell, 1990); and Hervieu-Léger, *Religion as a Chain of Memory* (n. 2, above). On the present discussion I strongly recommend a careful reading of Dale T. Irvin, *Christian Histories, Christian Traditioning: Rendering Accounts* (Maryknoll, N.Y.: Orbis Books, 1998).

13. Popular Catholicism is not strictly coextensive with the laity. It is no exaggeration, however, to affirm that popular Catholicism is and has been *mostly* created, practiced, and led by the laity, with or without hierarchical support (thus allowing for the inevitable exceptions). Particularly, women are and have been indispensable in creating and transmitting the formulations and expressions of popular Catholicism. Consequently, women have played a very significant role as *subjects* of the development of doctrine within Catholic tradition. I have more extensively discussed the role of women as bearers and subjects of tradition (with bibliography) in "An Exploration into the Theology of Grace and Sin," 121-52. In that same collection, María Pilar Aquino discusses the role of (Latina) women in tradition: "Theological Method in U.S. Latino/a Theology," 6-48. See also Michelle A. González, *"Nuestra Humanidad*: Toward a Latina Theological Anthropology," *Journal of Hispanic/Latino Theology* 8, no. 3 (2001): 49-72.

14. This is especially true of European American theologians of tradition, as evidenced by the recent (and otherwise excellent) works by Terrence

Tilley and John Thiel, cited in n. 1 above. If we searched the history of the theology of tradition, in the United States and in Europe, we will find only First-World perspectives presented and assumed as the exclusive or best Catholic interpretive lens by which to view tradition, as evidenced by publications (on diverse aspects of the theology of tradition) by such respected authors as Maurice Wiles, David Brown, Yves Congar, Karl Rahner, Joseph Ratzinger, Peter Lengsfeld, Johannes Feiner, Alois Stenzel, Karl Lehmann, and others. There are exceptions, of course. Among these are Robert Schreiter, Claude Geffré, and Siegfried Wiedenhofer. Let me also clarify here what I mean by the expressions "First World" and "Third World." By "First World" I mean the countries of the European Union, the United States, Canada, Australia, and New Zealand. By "Third World" I mean every other country on earth, but more specifically the nations of Latin America, Africa, and Asia, together with some of the countries that used to belong to the Soviet-led Eastern European bloc (formerly the "Second World"), as well as racial and/or ethnic minorities who are discriminated against in First-World nations. Any general description of these terms necessarily implies that there are exceptions.

15. The works of Third-World scholars in theology and philosophy are easily available, in Europe and the United States, through services such as the Aachen Institute of Missiology's annotated periodical bibliography, *Theology in Context*, which lists and abstracts articles from hundreds of academic journals, as well as books in theology and philosophy from across the Third World. Many European and American university libraries also have Third-World and First-World-minority scholarly works and journals in their collections. Availability, therefore, is not the reason for the absence of dialogue.

16. See Luciano Gruppi, *O conceito de hegemonia em Gramsci* (Rio de Janeiro: Edições Graal, 1978); Clodovis Boff, *Teoria do método teológico* (Petrópolis [Brazil]: Editora Vozes, 1998); Robert Young, *White Mythologies: Writing History and the West* (London: Routledge, 1990).

17. This point has been very forcefully argued by many of the theologians who participated in the international survey on the state of theology at the start of the third millennium, which was sponsored by Germany's Institute of Missiology. The results of that survey (which polled scholars Michael Amaladoss, Christian Duquoc, Gustavo Gutiérrez, Leonardo Boff, Johann B. Metz, Jürgen Moltmann, and many others with recognized scholarly reputations) can be found in Raúl Fornet-Betancourt, ed., *Theologie im III. Millennium: Antworten der Theologen. Dokumentation einer Weltumfrage* (Frankfurt a.M.: IKO/Verlag für Interkulturelle Kommunikation, 2000).

18. For what follows on globalization, I have relied especially on the following works: Barrie Axford, *The Global System: Economics, Politics and Culture* (New York: St. Martin's Press, 1995); Anthony Giddens, *The Consequences of Modernity* (Stanford, Calif.: Stanford University Press, 1990); Franz J. Hinkelammert, *Cultura de la esperanza y sociedad sin exclusión* (San José, Costa Rica: Editorial DEI, 1995); Peter Beyer, *Religion and Globalization* (London: SAGE Publications, 1994); James H. Mittelman, *The Globalization Syndrome: Transformation and Resistance* (Princeton, N.J.: Princeton University Press, 2000); Wim Dierckxsens, *Los límites de un capitalismo sin ciudadanía* (San José, Costa Rica: Editorial DEI, 1998); Raúl Fornet-Betancourt, ed., *Kapitalistische Globalisierung und Befreiung: Religiöse Erfahrungen und Option für das Leben* (Frankfurt a.M.: IKO/Verlag für Interkulturelle Kommunikation, 2000); Etienne Balibar and Immanuel Wallerstein, *Race, Nation, Class: Ambiguous Identities* (London: Verso, 1991); Rob Wilson and Wimal Dissanayake, eds., *Global/Local: Cultural Production and the Transnational Imaginary* (Durham, N.C.: Duke University Press, 1996); Santiago Castro-Gómez and Eduardo Mendieta, eds., *Teorías sin disciplina: Latinoamericanismo, poscolonialidad y globalización en debate* (Mexico City: Editorial Porrúa, 1998); Anthony B. King, ed., *Culture, Globalization, and the World-System* (Minneapolis, Minn.: University of Minnesota Press, 1997); Nelson Goodman, *Ways of Worldmaking* (Indianapolis, Ind.: Hackett, 1995); Ann Cvetkovich and Douglas Kellner, eds., *Articulating the Global and the Local: Globalization and Cultural Studies* (Boulder, Colo.: Westview Press, 1997); Saskia Sassen, *Guests and Aliens* (New York: New Press, 1999); Saskia Sassen, *Globalization and Its Discontents: Essays on the New Mobility of People and Money* (New York: New Press, 1998); Fredric Jameson and Masao Miyoshi, eds., *The Cultures of Globalization* (Durham, N.C.: Duke University Press, 1998).

19. Schreiter, *The New Catholicity* (n. 1, above), 5. See also Samuel P. Huntington, "The West: Unique, Not Universal," *Foreign Affairs* 75, no. 6 (1996): 28-46.

20. I readily acknowledge that, as a citizen of a First-World nation, I benefit from the dynamics and consequences of globalization, although I also acknowledge that, as a member of an ethnic-cultural minority in a First-World country, I belong to a community that can be (has been, and still is) the object of racist and other discriminatory prejudices. It would be unethical for me to claim to be in the same situation as theologians (and as the people in general) in most countries of the Third World; but it would be just as naive for me to think that First-World citizenship has brought the U.S.

Latino/a and African American communities real and effective equality in U.S. society (or within the U.S. church). Bigotry and racial stereotyping, unfortunately, are also globalized.

21. This, in my view, is a very serious critique which must be raised to European and especially to U.S. theologians who seem to engage postmodern philosophers without further consideration of the real-life consequences that such philosophers' theories might have on large portions of the world's populations (when the theories are appropriated, as they have been, by the ideological forces of globalization). Most Third-World scholars have strongly and consistently found significant ethical and theoretical lacunae (to put it mildly) in many of the postmodern philosophies which U.S. (and other) theologians use without prior rigorous ethical analysis. Simply as examples from Latin America, see Enrique Dussel, *Apel, Ricoeur, Rorty y la filosofía de la liberación* (Guadalajara, Mexico: Universidad de Guadalajara, 1993); Alfredo Gómez-Müller, "¿Qué universalidad para los derechos humanos?" *Cuadernos Latinoamericanos* 12 (2000): 1-21; Horacio Cerutti, *Filosofar desde nuestra América* (Mexico City: Editorial Porrúa, 2000); Dierckxsens, *Los límites de un capitalismo sin ciudadanía* (n. 18, above); Fornet-Betancourt, ed., *Kapitalistische Globalisierung und Befreiung* (with contributions by several Latin American scholars) (n. 18, above); Castro-Gómez and Mendieta, eds., *Teorías sin disciplina* (n. 18, above).

22. See Dierckxsens, *Los límites de un capitalismo sin ciudadanía.*

23. See Orlando O. Espín, "Immigration, Territory, and Globalization: Theological Reflections," *Journal of Hispanic/Latino Theology* 7, no. 3 (2000): 46-59; and idem, "La experiencia religiosa en el contexto de la globalización," *Journal of Hispanic/Latino Theology* 7, no. 2 (1999): 13-31.

24. See Espín, "Immigration, Territory, and Globalization: Theological Reflections" (n. 23, above); and idem, "La experiencia religiosa en el contexto de la globalización" (n. 23, above); Dierckxsens, *Los límites de un capitalismo sin ciudadanía* (n. 18, above); Cvetkovich and Kellner, eds., *Articulating the Global and the Local* (n. 18, above); Sassen, *Guests and Aliens* (n. 18, above); idem, *Globalization and Its Discontent* (n. 18, above).

25. See Espín, "Immigration, Territory, and Globalization" and "La experiencia religiosa en el contexto de la globalización" (n. 23, above), and the bibliography cited there.

26. The bibliography on immigration is immense. Merely as examples, see the excellent book by Saskia Sassen, *Globalization and Its Discontents* (n. 18, above); and also J. P. Smith and B. Edmonston, eds. *The New Americans: Economic, Demographic and Fiscal Effects of Immigration* (Washington,

D.C.: National Research Council, 1997); K. McCarthy and G. Vernez, *Immigration in a Changing Economy: California's Experience* (Santa Monica, Calif.: Rand Institute, 1997); M. M. Suárez-Orozco, ed., *Crossings: Mexican Immigration in Interdisciplinary Perspective* (Cambridge, Mass.: Harvard University Press, 1998); D. R. Maciel and M. Herrera-Sobek, eds., *Culture across Borders: Mexican Immigration and Popular Culture* (Tucson: University of Arizona Press, 1998). For a very good introduction to Catholic social teaching on immigration, as well as for an extensive bibliography on official Catholic views on immigration, see W. R. O'Neill and W. C. Spohn, "Rights of Passage: The Ethics of Immigration and Refugee Policy," *Theological Studies* 59, no. 1 (1998): 84-106.

27. See Hinkelammert, *Cultura de la esperanza y sociedad sin exclusión* (n. 18, above); Ana Sojo, *Mujer y política: Ensayo sobre el feminismo y el sujeto popular* (San José, Costa Rica: Editorial DEI, 1985); Andrés Serbin and Diego Ferreyra, eds., *Gobernabilidad democrática y seguridad ciudadana en Centroamérica: El caso de Nicaragua* (Managua: CRIES/Coordinadora Regional de Investigaciones Económicas y Sociales, 2000), and esp. the excellent paper by Dora María Téllez, "Nicaragua: Entorno económico y social," in *Gobernabilidad democrática y seguridad ciudadana en Centroamérica,* ed. Serbin and Ferreyra, 17-116.

28. See Axford, *The Global System* (n. 18, above); Mittelman, *The Globalization Syndrome* (n. 18, above); Wilson and Dissanayake, eds., *Global/Local* (n. 18, above); King, ed., *Culture, Globalization and the World-System* (n. 18, above); Cvetkovich and Kellner, eds., *Articulating the Global and the Local* (n. 18, above); Jameson and Miyoshi, eds., *The Cultures of Globalization,* (n. 18, above).

29. Although globalization is not identical to or coextensive with colonization, it would be naive (and analytically unacceptable) to ignore the myriad connections, mutual influences, and similarities between globalization and colonization, and indeed the evident colonizing thrust of globalization. I found postcolonial theory (recognizing its distinctive character and its own internal diversity) useful in further understanding globalization and its effects in the contemporary world. See Bart Moore-Gilbert, *Postcolonial Theory: Contexts, Practices, Politics* (London: Verso, 1997); Patrick Williams and Laura Chrisman, eds., *Colonial Discourse and Post-Colonial Theory* (New York: Columbia University Press, 1994); Ranajit Guha and Gayatri C. Spivak, eds., *Selected Subaltern Studies* (Oxford: Oxford University Press, 1988); Homi K. Bhabha, *The Location of Culture* (London: Routledge, 1994); Edward W. Said, *Orientalism* (New York: Vintage Books, 1979); Bill

Ashcroft, Gareth Griffiths, and Helen Tiffin, eds., *The Post-Colonial Studies Reader* (London: Routledge, 1995).

30. I occasionally suspect that some First-World theologians assume that their colleagues in the Third World (as well as minorities in the First World) are theologically "underdeveloped," in need of First-World "assistance" or "guidance" in becoming "sufficiently proficient" in professional theology. I suspect this because I have, in fact, heard such comments. I need not argue against such a colonial mentality. Its racist assumptions are morally and doctrinally unacceptable and unfounded, even when disguised under apparently "supportive" or "progressive" language. It is not surprising that many of those who display this attitude have rarely, if ever, taken the time to seriously study the publications and thought of the very authors they consider theologically "underdeveloped."

31. The International Society for Intercultural Philosophy was founded in 1992 (its statement of principles can be found in *Concordia. Internationale Zeitschrift für Philosophie* 23 [1993]: 127-28). Among the early works on intercultural thought, and solely as examples, see Raimón Pannikar, "La visió cosmoteándrica. El sentit religiós emergent del tercer milleni," *Qüestions de Vida Cristiana* 156 (1991): 78-102; H. Kimmerle, *Philosophie in Afrika: Annäherungen an einen interkulturellen Philosophiebegriff* (Frankfurt a.M.: IKO/Verlag Interkulturelle Kommunikation, 1991); F. Wimmer, *Interkulturelle Philosophie: Geschichte und Theorie,* 2 vols. (Vienna: Verso Verlag, 1990); Ram A. Mall, *Intercultural Philosophy* (London: Rowman & Littlefield, 2000) (a collection of earlier essays by the author that had appeared mostly in Germany, England, and India); Josef Estermann, "Hacia una filosofía del escuchar: Perspectivas de desarrollo para el pensamiento intercultural desde la tradición europea," in *Kulturen der Philosophie,* ed. R. Fornet-Betancourt (Frankfurt a.M.: IKO/Verlag Interkulturelle Kommunikation, 1996); Bollème, *El pueblo por escrito* (n. 3, above); David Sobrevilla, ed., *Filosofía de la cultura* (Madrid: Editorial Trotta, 1998); and the works by Raúl Fornet-Betancourt to which I refer below. On an earlier and still fascinating and pertinent model of intercultural thought, proposed by the late Argentinean philosopher Rodolfo Kusch, see Carlos M. Pagano Fernández, *Un modelo de filosofía intercultural: Rodolfo Kusch, 1922-1979* (Frankfurt a.M.: IKO/Verlag Interkulturelle Kommunikation, 1999).

32. Raúl Fornet-Betancourt has written extensively on the history of Latin American philosophies and their contributions. He has also published significant analyses of the philosophical work of Cuban thinker and patriot José Martí. Fornet-Betancourt's publications specifically on intercultural phi-

losophy and theology are extensive, and many have been translated into Spanish, Portuguese, German, and French, depending on the original language of publication. Among his works on intercultural thought are *Theologien in der Sozial- und Kulturgeschichte Lateinamerikas: Die perspektive der Arme. Band I. Interdisziplinäre und interkulturelle Forschung in der Theologie. Autochthone Theologien und Kulturen* (Eichstätt: Verlag des Katholische Universität, 1992); *Theologien in der Sozial- und Kulturgeschichte Lateinamerikas: Die perspektive der Arme. Band II. Theologien in der Praxis von Mission und Kolonialisierung. Ethnizität und nationale Kultur* (Eichstätt: Verlag des Katholische Universität, 1993); *Kulturen der Philosophie* (Frankfurt a.M.: IKO/Verlag Interkulturelle Kommunikation, 1996); *Lateinamerikanische Philosophie zwischen Inkulturation und Interkulturalität* (Frankfurt a.M.: IKO/Verlag Interkulturelle Kommunikation, 1997); "Aprender a filosofar desde el contexto de las culturas," *Revista de Filosofía* 90 (1997): 365-82; *Kapitalistische Globalisierung und Befreiung: Religiöse Erfahrungen und des Option für das Leben* (Frankfurt a.M.: IKO/Verlag Interkulturelle Kommunikation, 2000); "Aproximaciones a la globalización como universalización de políticas neoliberales, desde una perspectiva filosófica," *Revista Pasos* 83 (1998) (also available at www.dei-cr.org/pasos.htm#83); "La existencia como resistencia," *Concordia. Internationale Zeitschrift für Philosophie* 7 (1985): 95-101; and *Kulturen zwischen Tradition und Innovation* (Frankfurt a.M.: IKO/ Verlag Interkulturelle Kommunikation, 2001). In the present article, I have especially, but not exclusively, relied on Fornet-Betancourt's three best contributions (in his estimation and mine) on intercultural thought: *Interculturalidad y globalización: Ejercicios de crítica filosófica intercultural en el contexto de la globalización neoliberal* (Frankfurt a.M.: IKO/Verlag Interkulturelle Kommunikation, 2000); *Hacia una filosofía intercultural latinoamericana* (San José, Costa Rica: Editorial DEI, 1994); and *Transformación intercultural de la filosofía* (Bilbao: Editorial Desclée de Brouwer, 2001). Cuban-born Fornet-Betancourt is professor of philosophy at the University of Bremen and director of the Latin American section of the Institute of Missiology in Aachen.

33. See Raúl Fornet-Betancourt, *Hacia una filosofía intercultural latinoamericana*, 17-18, 33.

34. There are, evidently, other perspectives on inculturation, although they all admit the existence of a "canonical something." I view inculturation, consequently, as too close (or too open) to colonization. For a study of inculturation, which disagrees with my views, see Diego Irarrázaval, *Inculturation: New Dawn of the Church in Latin America* (Maryknoll, N.Y.: Orbis Books, 2000).

35. It should be noted that I am *not* proposing this "contrasting dialogue" only or mainly as an exercise among scholars. Faith communities are the key and indispensable subjects of the contrasting dialogue, aided by intellectuals to the degree that this aid might prove helpful to the communities' needs for dialogue. I should further add that Antonio Gramsci's notion of the "organic intellectual" is very pertinent when deciding who are the helpful scholars in the contrasting dialogue, as well as in determining the scholars' role therein. See Antonio Gramsci, *Literatura e vida nacional* (Rio de Janeiro: Editora Civilização Brasileira, 1978 [transl. of *Letteratura e vita nazionale*]); idem, *Concepção dialética da história* (Rio de Janeiro: Editora Civilização Brasileira, 1981 [transl. of *Il materialismo storico e la filosofia di Benedetto Croce*]); and idem, *Os intelectuais ea organização da cultura* (Rio de Janeiro: Editora Civilização Brasileira, 1979 [transl. of *Gli intellettuali e l'organizzazione della cultura*]).

36. See Raúl Fornet-Betancourt, *Hacia una filosofía intercultural latinoamericana*, 23-24.

37. Ibid, 24-25; idem, *Interculturalidad y globalización*, 14-17, 24-25, 27; idem, *Transformación intercultural de la filosofía*, 173-90, 273-84; and also Hervieu-Léger, *Religion as a Chain of Memory* (n. 2, above); Henri Lefebvre, *Critique de la vie quotidienne. I: Introduction* (Paris: L'Arche, 1958); Michel de Certeau, *La culture au pluriel* (Paris: Éditions du Seuil, 1994).

38. On "universal validity" and "universal relevance," see Espín, "An Exploration into the Theology of Grace and Sin," 121-52. See also Fornet-Betancourt, *Transformación intercultural de la filosofía*, 191-218, 273-84.

39. See Gruppi, *O conceito de hegemonia em Gramsci* (n. 16, above); Otto Maduro, *Religión y conflicto social* (Mexico City: Centro de Reflexión Teológica, 1980); Bhabha, *The Location of Culture* (n. 29, above). I found very fruitful the reflections on the construction of knowledge and truth (even religious truth) by philosopher Xavier Zubiri in *El problema filosófico de la historia de las religiones* (Madrid: Alianza Editorial/Fundación Xavier Zubiri, 1993), and idem, *Inteligencia sentiente: Inteligencia y realidad* (Madrid: Alianza Editorial/Fundación Xavier Zubiri, 1980).

40. See Gruppi, *O conceito de hegemonia em Gramsci* (n. 16, above); Hugues Portelli, *Gramsci et le bloc historique* (Paris: Presses Universitaires de France, 1972).

41. See Fornet-Betancourt, *Hacia una filosofía intercultural latinoamericana*, 25.

42. Fornet-Betancourt is highly critical of postmodern philosophers on several grounds, the most important of which is their apparent (theoretically

irresponsible) ethical naiveté in the context of globalization, as well as their apparent imperial disregard of substantive theoretical questions raised (for postmodern philosophies) by scholars from the Third World. The main works by Fornet-Betancourt (i.e., *Hacia una filosofía intercultural latinoamericana*, *Transformación intercultural de la filosofía*, and *Interculturalidad y globalización*, and especially the last named) are fierce in their critique of postmodern philosophies. Throughout the present article I have referred to postmodern philosophy on a number of occasions. The philosophies I have specifically in mind when making these comments on postmodernism are mainly (but not only) those of Richard Rorty and Donald Davidson. I have focused on these two philosophers because they seem to be the preferred dialogue partners of some of today's First-World theologians of tradition, especially U.S. theologians (but see below, in this same note, for other postmodern authors). Let this note stand as clarification for all references to postmodern philosophical thought in this paper, unless otherwise stated. For Richard Rorty, see *Philosophy and the Mirror of Nature* (Princeton, N.J.: Princeton University Press, 1979); *Philosophy and Social Hope* (London: Penguin Books, 1999); *Achieving Our Country* (Cambridge, Mass.: Harvard University Press, 1998); *Contingency, Irony, and Solidarity* (Cambridge: Cambridge University Press, 1989); *Objectivity, Relativism, and Truth: Philosophical Papers I* (Cambridge: Cambridge University Press, 1991); and *Truth and Progress: Philosophical Papers II* (Cambridge: Cambridge University Press, 1998). Engaging and critiquing Rorty is Norman Geras, *Solidarity in the Conversation of Humankind: The Ungroundable Liberalism of Richard Rorty* (London: Verso, 1995), as well as Dussel, *Apel, Ricoeur, Rorty y la filosofía de la liberación* (n. 21, above). Donald Davidson's bibliography is vast, and much of his most important thought is in his articles. The best introduction to his thought, with detailed listing of his works, and with significant essays on Davidson by other authors, is the massive volume edited by Lewis Edwin Hahn, *The Philosophy of Donald Davidson* (Chicago: Open Court, 1999). But see also, by Davidson, *Inquiries into Truth and Interpretation* (Oxford: Clarendon Press, 1984); and *Essays on Actions and Events* (Oxford: Clarendon Press, 1980). Evidently, postmodern thought is broader than Rorty's and Davidson's theories. For example, see Roland Barthes, *A Barthes Reader* (London: Fontana, 1982); Jean Baudrillard, *Selected Writings* (Cambridge: Polity Publishers, 1988); Jacques Derrida, *Writing and Difference* (Chicago: University of Chicago Press, 1967); idem, *Margins of Philosophy* (Chicago: University of Chicago Press, 1972); idem, *Glas* (Lincoln: University of Nebraska Press, 1974); idem, "Living on: borderlines," in *Deconstruction and Criticism,* ed. Harold Bloom et al. (London: Routledge

& Kegan Paul, 1979), 75-176; idem, *The Post Card: From Socrates to Freud and Beyond* (Chicago: University of Chicago Press, 1980); idem, *Spectres of Marx: The State of Debt, the Work of Mourning, and the New International* (London: Routledge, 1993); Terry Eagleton, *The Crisis of Contemporary Culture* (Oxford: Clarendon Press, 1993); Jean-François Lyotard, *La Condition postmoderne: Rapport sur le savoir* (Paris: Minuit, 1979); idem, *Le Postmoderne expliqué aux enfants: Corréspondence, 1982-1985* (Paris: Galilée, 1986).

43. By "need" here, I want to say "requirement," "condition," or "demand sine qua non," or some such ethical obligation. I am not assuming, however, a universally valid principle or ethical "essence" or moral imperative underlying the obligation; rather, I am referring to the internal need of particularities (perceived precisely as need by and within the particularities) for their own ethical subsistence and coherence.

44. Raúl Fornet-Betancourt, in *Hacia una filosofía intercultural latinoamericana*, arrives at a very clear and emphatic conclusion: "El mismo posmodernismo particularista, al decretar que no existe más nada fuera o más allá de sí, no hace sino repetir de modo aparentemente nuevo la misma mentalidad occidental colonizante que decreta que su particularidad es la verdadera universalidad. El posmodernismo particularista no es más que la nueva faz de la colonización, que establece al Occidente como quien tiene y conoce la verdad de manera mejor, más clarividente y convincente" (p. 38). See also idem, *Interculturalidad y globalización*, 83-84 (n. 32, above).

45. See Geras, *Solidarity in the Conversation of Humankind* (n. 42, above).

46. This has been a repeated theme in the writings of Roberto S. Goizueta and María Pilar Aquino. See, for instance, by Goizueta, *Caminemos con Jesús* (n. 4, above), as well as his article "Fiesta: Life in the Subjunctive," in *From the Heart of Our People,* ed. Espín and Díaz, 84-99 (n. 4, above). Aquino's article in that same volume ("Theological Method in U.S. Latino/a Theology: Toward an Intercultural Theology for the Third Millennium," 6-48) is an example of this critique of postmodernist philosophical thought.

47. See Said, *Orientalism* (n. 29, above); Young, *White Mythologies* (n. 16, above); Fredric Jameson, *Postmodernism, or, The Cultural Logic of Late Capitalism* (Durham, N.C.: Duke University Press, 1997).

48. On "foundationalism" and "nonfoundationalism," see John E. Thiel, *Nonfoundationalism* (Minneapolis, Minn.: Fortress Press, 1994), as well as the books by Thiel (*Senses of Tradition*) and Tilley (*Inventing Catholic Tradition*), cited in n. 1 above. See also Matthias Steup, *An Introduction to Contemporary Epistemology* (Upper Saddle River, N.J.: Prentice Hall, 1996); Mary E. John, *Discrepant Dislocations: Feminism, Theory, and Postcolonial Histories* (Berkeley,

Calif.: University of California Press, 1996); and Seyla Benhabib, Judith Butler, Drucilla Cornell, and Nancy Fraser, *Feminist Contentions: A Philosophical Exchange* (New York: Routledge, 1995), especially Judith Butler's essay, "Contingent Foundations: Feminism and the Question of 'Postmodernism,'" 35-58.

49. See Fornet-Betancourt, *Hacia una filosofía intercultural latinoamericana*, 34-35; idem, *Interculturalidad y globalización*, 33-39.

50. I have no doubt that Richard Rorty believes his philosophy to be sufficient for worldwide solidarity. And he insists on this in several of his books. But he has been unable or unwilling to significantly acknowledge and respond to his Third-World critics. His main attempt at responding was his *Hope Instead of Knowledge*, which, for the most part, repeats earlier arguments, and which addresses, not surprisingly, mainly European critiques of his work. Some of his replies to criticism have seemed too superficial to many across the Third World and in Europe, and Rorty has been outright dismissive of much of this critique. For an illuminating insight into Rorty's motives, reason, and theories, see Derek Nystrom and Kent Puckett, *Against Bosses, Against Oligarchies: A Conversation with Richard Rorty* (Charlottesville, Va.: Prickly Pear Pamphlets, 1998).

51. See Fornet-Betancourt, *Interculturalidad y globalización*, 151-53; idem, *Transformación intercultural de la filosofía*, 173-218.

52. See Fornet-Betancourt, *Hacia una filosofía intercultural latinoamericana*, 36-38, 73-98; idem, *Interculturalidad y globalización*, 9-20, 51-58.

53. In the theology of tradition, the usual "objects of study," or sources, have been the Bible, ecclesial creeds, decisions and definitions by ecumenical councils, the works of the early bishops and theologians of the church (patristics), the *sensus fidelium*, statements by the episcopal and papal magisterium, the works of medieval and post-Reformation/post-Tridentine theologians (all the way to more contemporary authors), and, especially since the mid-nineteenth century, the history of the development of doctrine. I have proposed, in this article and elsewhere (e.g., *The Faith of the People*), that popular Catholicism be included in the list of sources. An intercultural theology of tradition would include all of the above, as well as the cultural perspectives and experiences of Catholic communities worldwide engaged in the significant "contrasting" dialogue which would yield the universally relevant truth(s) which can be labeled as "tradition" by the Catholic faith communities. These faith communities, because they exist only in specific cultures, have produced their own "theologizing subjects" (communities and individuals in communities). The notion of theologizing subjects is closely related, but not identical, to Antonio Gramsci's notion of the "organic intel-

lectuals." On Gramsci's "organic intellectuals" see the bibliography in notes 35 and 40, above.

54. See Fornet-Betancourt, *Interculturalidad y globalización*, 99-106; John, *Discrepant Dislocations* (n. 48, above).

55. See Fornet-Betancourt, *Hacia una filosofía intercultural latinoamericana*, 23-31, 51-60.

56. See Fornet-Betancourt, *Interculturalidad y globalización*, 12-17; idem, *Transformación intercultural de la filosofía*, 173-218.

57. See Manuel J. Mejido, "A Critique of the 'Aesthetic Turn' in U.S. Hispanic Theology: A Dialogue with Roberto Goizueta and the Positing of a New Paradigm," *Journal of Hispanic/Latino Theology* 8, no. 3 (2001): 18-48. In this article, Mejido makes a very valid argument for grounding theology on social conditions and reality; yet his reading and evaluation of Goizueta's work do not convince and seem biased.

58. See Orlando O. Espín, "Mexican Religious Practices, Popular Catholicism, and the Development of Doctrine," in *Horizons of the Sacred: Mexican Traditions in U.S. Catholicism*, ed. Timothy Matovina and Gary Riebe-Estrella (Ithaca, N.Y.: Cornell University Press, 2002). See also Fornet-Betancourt, *Interculturalidad y globalización*, 13-50; and idem, *Kulturen zwischen Tradition und Innovation* (n. 6, above).

59. See Fornet-Betancourt, *Transformación intercultural de la filosofía*, 285-98, 349-70.

60. See Ignacio Ellacuría, *Filosofía de la realidad histórica* (Madrid: Editorial Trotta, 1991); and Kevin F. Burke, *The Ground Beneath the Cross: The Theology of Ignacio Ellacuría* (Washington, D.C.: Georgetown University Press, 2000), which includes a complete bibliography of Ellacuría's works in philosophy and theology. See also Juan Antonio Senent de Frutos, *Ellacuría y los derechos humanos* (Bilbao: Editorial Desclée de Brouwer, 1998); and Jordi Corominas, *Ética primera: Aportación de X. Zubiri al debate ético contemporáneo* (Bilbao: Desclée de Brouwer, 1999).

61. See Fornet-Betancourt, *Interculturalidad y globalización*, 25-50; Enrique Dussel, *Arquitectónica de una ética de la liberación en la edad de la globalización y la exclusión* (Mexico City: Siglo XXI Editores, 1998), esp. chap. 6; José Ortega y Gasset, *Meditaciones del Quijote* (Madrid: Editorial Espasa-Calpe, 1964); Gruppi, *O conceito de hegemonia em Gramsci* (n. 16, above); Portelli, *Gramsci et le bloc historique* (n. 40, above); Mary McCanney Gergen, ed., *Feminist Thought and the Structure of Knowledge* (New York: New York University Press, 1988); Samuel Fleischacker, *The Ethics of Culture* (Ithaca, N.Y.: Cornell University Press, 1994).

62. See Raúl Fornet-Betancourt, *Interculturalidad y globalización*, 26-27: "La cultura es la *situación* de la condición humana, y no la condición humana misma. Para el ser humano no hay uso de la libertad ni tampoco de la razón sin condicionamiento cultural, pero tampoco hay cultura humana sin la praxis de la libertad ni el ejercicio reflexivo de la razón. . . . Existe un conflicto de tradiciones e interpretaciones en el seno mismo de cada cultura y, por consiguiente, en cada proceso de diálogo e interacción intercultural. Todo universo cultural conlleva la tensión entre opresión y liberación."

63. I think my affirmation is close to Walter Kasper's frequently repeated thought that the universal church exists in and consists of local churches. Kasper, of course, reminds us that the Second Vatican Council (*Lumen Gentium* 23) teaches this, as well as the Eastern Orthodox and Anglican traditions. See Walter Kasper, *Theology and Church* (New York: Crossroad, 1989), 156-65; idem, "On the Church: A Friendly Reply to Cardinal Ratzinger," *America* 184, no. 14 (April 23-30, 2001): 8-14; and especially his "Das Zweite Vatikanum weiterdenken: Die apostolische Sukzession im Bischofsamt als ökumenisches Problem," *Kerygma und Dogma* 44, no. 3 (1998): 207-18.

64. U.S. Latino/a Catholic theologians have been arguing this point for almost two decades. And so have African American Catholic theologians. A very important collection of essays in this regard (and by no means the only publication on the topic) is the December 2000 issue of *Theological Studies*, which was dedicated to the Catholic reception of black theology in the United States. Within that issue, the essays by M. Shawn Copeland ("Tradition and the Traditions of African American Catholicism" [n. 1, above]) and by Bryan N. Massingale ("James Cone and Recent Catholic Episcopal Teaching on Racism," 700-730) are extremely pertinent to the subject of the present article and to the point I just made in the text. More specifically, I find Copeland's essay especially rich in "contrasting" intercultural dialogue with the European American and U.S. Latino/a communities and theologies, although she never uses the terminology of intercultural theory. In "re-perspectivizing" African American popular Catholicism, as well as in arguing for the universal relevance of African American Catholic understanding(s) and experience(s) of tradition, Copeland demonstrates the richness and potential of intercultural "contrasting dialogue." Her text further evidences her awareness of and conversation with U.S. Latino/a contributions to the theology of tradition, once again demonstrating the pertinence of intercultural dialogue and theory in U.S. theology. As an important and very relevant aside, U.S. Latino/a Catholic theologians must pay much closer attention to the scholarly works being elaborated by our African American

Catholic colleagues. It is increasingly unacceptable to speak of intercultural dialogue, *mestizaje*, etc., and yet dismiss the African American Catholic communities as if they were not our (i.e., Latinos/as) most obvious *and* indispensable dialogue partners. Copeland made the same point on the need for collaboration in a paper presented at the 2001 national convention of the Catholic Theological Society of America, in Milwaukee ("Racism and the Vocation of the Theologian"). See also Zipporah G. Glass, "The Language of *Mestizaje* in a Renewed Rhetoric of Black Theology," *Journal of Hispanic/Latino Theology* 7, no. 2 (1999): 32-42.

65. As examples, see José M. de Paiva, *Colonização e catequese* (São Paulo: Cortez Editora, 1982); and Luis N. Rivera, *A Violent Evangelism: The Political and Religious Conquest of the Americas* (Louisville, Ky.: Westminster John Knox Press, 1992).

66. See Kasper, "Das Zweite Vatikanum weiterdenken" (n. 63, above).

67. See Kasper, *Theology and Church*, 156-65; idem, "On the Church," 8-14; idem, "Das Zweite Vatikanum."

68. See Espín, "Mexican Religious Practices, Popular Catholicism, and the Development of Doctrine" (n. 58, above); and Thiel, *Senses of Tradition* (n. 1, above).

69. See Espín, *The Faith of the People* (n. 4, above), esp. chap. 3, on the relationship between the *sensus fidelium* and popular Catholicism; Daniel J. Finucane, *Sensus Fidelium: The Use of a Concept in the Post-Vatican II Era* (Bethesda, Md.: International Scholars Publications, 1996); Walter Kasper, "Das Verhältnis von Schrift und Tradition: Eine Pneumatologische Perspektive," *Theologische Quartalschrift* 170 (1990): 161-90.

70. When I affirm in the present article that popular Catholicism is the *ordinary* way of judging the legitimacy of any claim to continuity and legitimacy in the tradition, I do not mean to imply by "ordinary" any more than "most frequent." The reason for this seems evident: the immense majority of Catholics and Catholic communities throughout the world live their faith in the overall style described here by me and others as popular Catholicism. I am not assuming either that popular Catholicism is the same throughout the world, because it is not. See Copeland, "Tradition and the Traditions of African American Catholics" (n. 1, above); Espín, *The Faith of the People* (n. 4, above); idem, "An Exploration into the Theology of Grace and Sin" (n. 12, above); Bamat and Wiest, eds., *Popular Catholicism in a World Church* (n. 5, above).

71. I convincingly argued for this intimate connection between the *sensus fidelium* and popular Catholicism in chap. 3 of *The Faith of the People*.

72. See Kasper, *Theology and Church*, 156-65; idem, "On the Church," 8-14.

73. In addition to the works already mentioned in the several bibliographical notes on popular Catholicism, see also, from a vast body of literature on the subject, José O'Callaghan, *El cristianismo popular en el antiguo Egipto* (Salamanca: Ediciones Sígueme, 1980); Robert A. Orsi, *The Madonna of 115th Street: Faith and Community in Italian Harlem, 1880-1950* (New Haven, Conn.: Yale University Press, 1985); Nicholas Perry and Loreto Echeverría, *Under the Heel of Mary* (London: Routledge, 1988); Peter Brown, *The Cut of the Saints: Its Rise and Function in Latin Christianity* (Chicago: University of Chicago Press, 1981); Duffy, *The Stripping of the Altars* (n. 5, above); and Rosalind and Christopher Brooke, *Popular Religion in the Middle Ages* (London: Thames and Hudson, 1984).

74. See Kasper, "Das Verhältnis von Schrift und Tradition" (n. 69, above); Heinrich Fries, "La revelación," in *Mysterium Salutis,* ed. Johannes Feiner and Magnus Löhrer (Madrid: Ediciones Cristiandad, 1969), 1:207-85; Peter Lengsfeld and Herbert Haag, "La presencia de la revelación en la Escritura y en la Tradición," in *Mysterium Salutis,* ed. Feiner and Löhrer, 1:287-557; Johannes Feiner, Magnus Löhrer, Basil Studer, Alois Stenzel, Karl Rahner, Karl Lehmann, and Hans Urs von Balthasar, "La presencia de la revelación por medio de la Iglesia," in *Mysterium Salutis,* 559-859; Yves Congar, *Tradition and Traditions* (New York: Macmillan, 1967); Josef R. Geiselmann, *The Meaning of Tradition* (New York: Herder & Herder, 1966); Karl Rahner and Josef Ratzinger, *Revelation and Tradition* (New York: Herder & Herder, 1966); Karl Rahner, *Foundations of Christian Faith* (New York: Crossroad, 1985), 138-75, 369-78; Heinrich Fries, "Fortschritt und Tradition," *Stimmen der Zeit* 193 (1975): 75-89.

75. On the fear of relativism, read *again,* Gruppi, *O conceito de hegemonia em Gramsci* (n. 16, above); Peter L. Berger and Thomas Luckmann, *The Social Construction of Reality* (New York: Doubleday/Anchor, 1967); Peter L. Berger, *The Sacred Canopy* (New York: Doubleday/Anchor, 1969); Gianni Vattimo, *Creer que se cree* (Barcelona: Paidós, 1996); Gabriel Marcel, *Homo viator* (Paris: Éditions Montaigne, 1945); idem, *Du refus a l'invocation* (Paris: Éditions Gallimard, 1964); Albert Camus, "The Just Assassins," in *Caligula and Three Other Plays,* by Albert Camus (New York: Vintage Books, 1968); Paul Ricoeur, *O conflito das interpretações. Ensaios de hermenêutica* (Rio de Janeiro: Imago Editora, 1978); idem, *History and Truth* (Evanston, Ill.: Northwestern University Press, 1965).

76. Studies that analyze the several forms that the papal and episcopal

magisterium has taken throughout the history of the church are too many to list here. It is very well attested, in history and in scholarly research, that the current magisterial forms, styles, and practices are not necessary. Although the papal and episcopal magisterium is essential to Catholicism, the forms, styles, and practices of their concrete historical implementation or expression are not. John Paul II has said as much in his encyclical *Ut unum sint* (1995). The questions I raise about the text refer explicitly to the possible implementation or expression of the episcopal and papal magisterium in an intercultural model and context. Not much has been written on ecclesiology and ecclesiological models from an intercultural perspective. Of interest in constructing a reply to the questions raised are the following: Peter Hünermann, "Amt und Evangelium: Die Gestalt des Petrusdienstes am Ende des zweiten Jahrstausends," *Herder Korrespondenz* 50 (1996): 298-302; Jürgen Moltmann, "Ökumene im Zeitalter der Globalisierungen: Die Enzyklika 'Ut unum sint' im evangelischer Sicht," *Evangelische Theologie* 58 (1998): 262-69; Paul Tihon, "Por une nouvelle 'catholicité' ecclésiale," *Recherches de Science Religieuse* 86 (1998): 123-42; and Kasper, "Das Zweite Vatikanum weiterdenken" (n. 63, above). Very important in this discussion is Robert J. Schreiter's book, *Constructing Local Theologies* (Maryknoll, N.Y.: Orbis Books, 1985). It might prove very useful for Catholic theologians of tradition to seriously consider recent contributions by Anglican theologians in Britain and in the United States to a broader and authentic understanding of *Catholic* tradition; see Brown, *Tradition and Imagination* (n. 1, above), as well as *Anglican Theological Review* 82, no. 4 (2000), which was entirely dedicated to this topic.

77. For a brief history of the theology of grace, see Piet Fransen, "Desarrollo histórico de la doctrina de la gracia," in *Mysterium Salutis*, ed. Feiner and Löhrer, IV/2, 611-730. See also Orlando O. Espín, "Grace and Humanness," in *We Are a People! Initiatives in Hispanic American Theology,* ed. Roberto S. Goizueta (Minneapolis, Minn.: Fortress Press, 1992), 133-64; Martín Gelabert Ballester, *Salvación como humanización: Esbozo de una teología de la gracia* (Madrid: Ediciones Paulinas, 1985); Mário de França Miranda, *Libertados para a práxis da justiça. A teologia da graça no atual contexto latino-americano* (São Paulo: Edições Loyola, 1980).

78. See Walter Kasper, *Theology and Church*, 156-65; and on a similar but ecumenical note, idem, "Lo stato del dialogo ecumenico fra Chiesa cattolica e Chiese della Riforma," *Asprenas* 29, no. 1 (1982): 3-12.

2

Humanitas, Identity, and Another Theological Anthropology of (Catholic) Tradition

The question that has typically driven theological anthropology has been What is the human person? This question has sought not merely philosophical but also explicitly theological answers, assuming, as Christian theology must, that Jesus the Christ has profoundly and forever affected what we can understand as humanness. The answer to What is the human person? could be attempted (and has frequently been attempted) through analytical, relational, or phenomenological categories that have often led to generic answers that, in turn, paint a generic human, and an equally generic *humanitas*, that might exist in theory but not in real life. But we know all too well that neither humans nor *humanitas* can be or has ever been generic or theoretical.[1]

Perhaps theological anthropology's typical driving question needs reconsideration. Perhaps instead of *What* is the human person? we should be asking *Who* are human persons?[2] The latter

This is the text of a paper presented at the 2006 national colloquium of the Academy of Catholic Hispanic Theologians of the U.S. (ACHTUS). This particular meeting, in San Antonio, Texas, gathered together members of ACHTUS and members of the Black Catholic Theological Symposium (BCTS). My paper was presented in dialogue with a paper by M. Shawn Copeland in the general session on theological anthropology. All papers in the annual ACHTUS colloquia are intended to provoke debate and conversation. A variation of the present text appeared in the *E-Journal of Hispanic/Latino Theology* (www.latinotheology.org).

question discloses real life, real persons, and real communities, while the former, at best, discloses theories. I am aware that I am not the first one to propose this reconsideration, and I know I will not be the last, but given our colloquium's general theme, it seems an important enough issue to again bring to our collective attention.[3]

In order to help me justify this proposal, I will begin by sharing some important reflections on identity and on what I here call *humanitas*, because identity and *humanitas* lie at the heart of most issues in theological anthropology. I will then proceed with some suggestions as to what a change in theological anthropology's driving question would imply. And I will conclude with the application of (or perhaps a "passionate" reflection on) the question *Who* are human persons? to an unavoidable civil- and human-rights situation in our world today that both Latina/o and black Catholic theologies and theologians have, for the most part, ignored.

The purpose of this paper is to raise some questions regarding theological anthropology and, perhaps more uncomfortably, to ask why our black and Latina/o theologies have been silent and absent from one of the more important civil- and human-rights struggles of our day. I hope to raise the questions and make us feel sufficiently uncomfortable to provoke our engagement.

Humanitas and Identity

By *humanitas* I do *not* mean simply or mainly "humanity" as the sum of all human persons in history or at any one point in history (i.e., *humanitas*, here, is not a synonym for "human race"). By *humanitas,* I mean that which we share and recognize in persons and communities—that is, that living, historical, complex reality that allows us to then speak of "humanity" but that first allows us to point to a being and to a community and label them as "human." *Humanitas*, it seems to me, identifies the most crucial of theologically anthropological questions.

Humanitas is not historically a quality that exists apart from or prior to or "underneath" specifically and diversely contextualized persons or communities; *humanitas* exists only in and through real persons and communities, not as a pre- or ahistorical substratum underlying "person" and "community" but as *the living, dynamic intersection of real-life diverse contextualizations, which exists only and when that living intersection historically exists.*

Humanitas has never existed, therefore, as a generic "nature,"[4] but as the intersection of specific, living, and diverse contextualizations that recognizes another as human precisely *because* it recognizes in the other the historical, living reality of unfolding specific and diverse contextualizations that humans have constructed, and continue to construct, in history. *Humanitas,* therefore, implies identity: our own and that of others. *Humanitas,* furthermore, can be best recognized interculturally in others.[5]

Humanitas exists only in and through real-life humans. It has never actually existed in theory, even in those theories we might judge to be good, competent explanations or descriptions of *humanitas.* Humans are always contextual, when understood either as individuals or as members of communities, or as communities themselves.

Consequently*, humanitas only exists if and when contextual.* There is no precontextual or a-contextual *humanitas.* Contextualization, therefore, is not adjacent or added to *humanitas* but, rather, contextualization is the very sine qua non condition of *humanitas.*

The contextualized historical reality of *humanitas* is never monochrome or simple. Contextualization is always complex, plurichrome, and multiple, intersecting in, and thereby producing, a vast array of human differences. *Humanitas* is thus not only contextual but also diverse; and just as contextualization is not adjacent or added to *humanitas* but a sine qua non condition for it, so is diversity a sine qua non condition of *humanitas.* Contextual diversity or diverse contextualization: without these there has never been and there can never be *humanitas* (except in a generic theory that, because of its being generic and because of its being theory, cannot be real-life *humanitas*).

Contextualization and diversity define *humanitas*. Thus, they define human identity too. These diverse contextualizations (or these contextual diversities) thus richly define *humanitas*. I am thinking of genders, cultures, races, sexual orientations, social classes, social positions, and so on.[6] These all intersect, individually and communally, to define who human persons and their communities are. We are not one or another of these contextualizations, but the dynamic, living, historical intersection (and not necessarily synthesis) of them as these unveil themselves in ourselves.

We *are* our diverse, living contextualizations, and we can affirm that "we are we" (and I can affirm that "I am I"); hence, we can affirm an explicit identity as we arrive at and become the naming and the assuming ("self-disclosing") of the diverse contextualizations that (by their specific, living intersection) shaped and defined (and continue to shape and define) who we are before we ever named or assumed them. Our identities (individual and communal) are the historical, intersectional unfolding of our specific and diverse contextualizations: "are" and not just "result from."

Identity can be said to be the process of recognition of self in community, of "disclosing" my self to myself and others, as "my"/ "our" diverse, living, and contextual *humanitas* (in a specific way— i.e., at the point of intersection of our always-present diverse contextualizations). Identity is the recognition or self-disclosure that names *who* we are, and it is always *ours;* and because it is "ours," it is not a single-instant act but a historical process. *We* are *not* a single-act act but beings that *become* who we *are* in historical processes.[7]

"I/we are human" can only mean that I/we are human in, through, and because of *this* specific, living, diverse, and contextual process or manner of *humanitas* which is defined by the living intersection of diverse contextualizations of gender, race, culture, social class, social position, sexual orientation, and so on. We cannot define ourselves or claim an identity as humans in generic terms because only specifically and diversely contextualized humans exist. Furthermore, our identities exist within broader historical, conflictive situations within which these identities can and do play, or can be made to play, roles that might lead to social outcomes not always supportive or reflective of who we are.

This is why (among other reasons) the driving question for theological anthropology should not be "what" is the human person but "who." Because the driving question of theological anthropology cannot address a generic being or a theory, it should address the living, real human; and hence, theological anthropology should also address the issue of the living intersections of diverse contextualizations (and the contextualizations themselves), and their role as definer of true *humanitas.*

Another Theological Anthropology

If it is true that humans and, consequently, *humanitas* and human identities can only be human *in* and *as* the real-life, historical intersections of diverse contextualizations, then one could ask if theological anthropology can exist as the discipline that simply or mainly asks What is the human person?

Because there is no generic human person, can there be a discipline that asks about human persons generically and attempts to reply also generically? Of course not. This does not mean, however, that there can be no theological anthropology, or that theological theory is useless or necessarily suspect. Not at all! But if theological anthropology were to ask Who are human persons?, in the plural, thereby acknowledging our necessary human diversity, then we might open the door to another, more historically realistic theological anthropology and a more ethical theological theory.[8]

The moment we ask Who are human persons? in historical reality, which is the only reality that exists, then we have to deal with and squarely face issues of power and of power asymmetries, issues of domination and hegemony, issues of manipulation and alienation, and issues of sin and grace as these exist, are dynamically intertwined, and as they are contextualized in the real human world. To ask Who are human persons? necessarily leads to unmasking all sorts of unethical options and perspectives that often underlie theological reflection and suck the prophetic and the ethical from its constructs.[9]

If we ask Who are human persons?, and ask this within real life, we are confronted with questions regarding those who have been, and still are, regarded as nonhuman, as lacking in *humanitas*, as secondarily human, or as human in a derived way. To ask Who are human persons? triggers, therefore, political and ethical judgments and demands answers to questions of equality and justice.[10]

This alternative way of asking the driving anthropological question can become dangerous and prophetic. This is illustrated in Christian history in the blunt sermons in Santo Domingo of Antonio de Montesinos ("Are these not human?") as well as in the extraordinarily fierce sermons in Havana and Caracas of Francisco José de Jaca and Epifanio Moiráns ("Have you no eyes with which to see that they are your brothers and sisters?"). Montesinos,[11] for his defense of Taíno natives, and Jaca and Moiráns[12] for their stand against black slavery, paid dearly for daring to ask Who are human persons? and for seeing in the conquered and enslaved the evident *humanitas* they recognized in themselves.[13] Their persecutors, nevertheless, understood very well that to raise the issue of "who" is human was a political and ethical affront to the dominant social system.

U.S. Latina/o and black theologies have much in common, just as they also have much to legitimately distinguish them. Among their commonalities is the passion for justice and, more specifically, the passion for recognizing evident *humanitas* in most human persons. And yes, I just said "most" and not "all" human persons.

In the name of our shared passion for justice, I dare here to call to our attention a silence and absence in our theologies and, in particular, one increasingly glaring absence and silence. Although Latina/o and black theologians would be adamant in stating that our shared commitment for justice, equality, and liberation is for the benefit of *all,* in real life (and, again, real life is the only life we have) our silences and absences might suggest that we too make exceptions.

I understand that our numbers impose limitations on our work; we cannot say or do everything that we know needs to be said or done. There are not enough black or Latina/o Catholic theologians to reflect seriously on all that requires their professional attention. I realize that; and it is a legitimate point to bring up in our defense. Our numbers impose silences and absences we wished were otherwise. But the silences and absences I have in mind have more to do with our choices, our fears, and our prejudices than with our lack of numbers. These silences and absences might be partially blinding our passion for justice, and perhaps aiding our own domestication as "acceptable" academics.

Allow me one example in order to illustrate our silences and absences, and how our passion for justice has not extended the recognition of evident *humanitas* to all because we have made exceptions, in fact if not in intention, when answering Who are human persons? Unfortunately, there are other examples—I wish there were none!—and the one I bring to your attention is uncomfortable enough for most Latina/o and black theologians, but precisely because of that, it will make my point. I bring to your attention our silences and absences in relation to the Latina/o and black LGBT (lesbian, gay, bisexual, and transgender) communities.

In keeping with the usual manner of discussing issues in standard Catholic theology, it should be noted that in this paper I am not discussing the ethics of homosexual acts but the fact that homosexuals, regardless of everything else, are human persons and, as a necessary consequence of this (in keeping with standard Catholic theology), are bearers of human dignity and inalienable rights given them by the creator and not dependent for that dignity and those inalienable rights on civil or canonical legislation. As a further necessary consequence, and again in keeping with standard Catholic theology, no violation of human dignity and of the God-given inalienable rights of human persons (LGBT persons evidently included) may be ever permitted by Catholic ethics.

Another Theological Anthropology: The *Humanitas* of the Latina/o and Black LGBT Communities

A number of Latina/o and black Catholic theologians have listed heterosexism and homophobia as evils symptomatic of wider and deeper social oppression. But most often, in our writings, these statements appear as part of longer lists of evil symptoms and not as the main focus of our papers, articles, or books.[14] I am not disregarding or downplaying what has been written or said, but I don't think we can hold that a few phrases—no matter how accurate, passionate, and sincere—are sufficient. We have been mostly silent on the topic, at least within the world of the Catholic theological academy. And on this we have been absent too within our Latina/o and black communities, and especially absent among and to LGBT Latinas/os and blacks.

I am not saying or suggesting that all Latina/o and black theologians are homophobic. I know that most of us are not. And yet, the topic seems to be so untouchable that, in fact, we have not reflected on it at length within our respective theologies, and mere inclusion in a passing phrase does not qualify as sustained reflection. Why hasn't our interpersonal inclusiveness, which we do show one another, regardless of sexual orientation, led to public theological reflection on LGBT black and Latina/o persons and their plight in society?

I cannot believe that black and Latina/o theologians have nothing significant to say about heterosexism and about homophobia. I cannot believe that we have so little to say to people in our own communities who are mistreated, abused, persecuted by our own communities, churches, and theologies, and, in the best of cases, forced to hide who they are! We theologians have been silent and absent, for all practical purposes, on an increasingly important social issue that rests completely on our answer to a crucial theological question: Who are human persons?

Our silences and absences are perhaps providing unexpected loud answers that we might not want to live with. Our silences and absences might be indicative of exceptions we have made in our inclusiveness and in our struggles for justice for all, exceptions possibly made out of fear of provoking our own repression. Our silences and absences seem to be telling black and Latina/o LGBT persons that they are not quite as equal or important in rights, in *humanitas,* and in our priorities as other oppressed communities are. We seem to be telling them that on the scales of suffering, theirs does not weigh much. We seem to be suggesting that the threats of persecutors are more important to us than the cry of the victims.

Are black and Latina/o LGBT persons "human" too? "Are these not humans?" if I may quote from Antonio de Montesinos's sermon on the first Sunday of Advent, 1511.[15] And if they are, where have we been when they are persecuted and vilified in the name of God and doctrine, hence, in the name of theology—in *our* name, because we are theologians?[16] Where has been our passionate defense of the dignity and *humanitas* of *all?* Have we too been making exceptions and distinctions among persons based on sexual orientation and on our fears and prejudices, thereby making ourselves somehow complicit with oppression? Have the interests of the dominant in church and society become a deciding factor in our theological scholarship, leading us to censor ourselves? Are we so afraid of being persecuted for speaking evident truth (i.e., for publicly affirming the evident *humanitas* of LGBT persons) that we have been willing to ignore the plight of thousands, if not millions, of Latinas/os and blacks?

If we give ourselves permission to discriminate against others, and to play down or silence their existence and suffering in our theologies, how can we then morally justify our insistence that European American theologians not play down or silence us and our communities in their theologies, and not discriminate against us in their institutions and in society at large?

We cannot stand for such a double standard. It is clear, given our silences and absences, that most of us have chosen to avoid any public connection with the lives, contributions, and oppression of LGBT Latinas/os and blacks, even when in private many of us do respect and even cherish them.

Or do we think it is perfectly moral to allow the oppression of some in order to preserve the credibility of our theological scholarship in the eyes of the dominant? In the name of the Christian God? We, the daughters and sons of those who in our country's history have suffered terribly because of such exceptions made by otherwise good Christians, should be profoundly disgusted at the mere insinuation that as theologians we could do unto others what has been done, and continues to be done, unto us.

Am I bringing up our silences and absences in reference to the LGBT community because it might be the "oppression *du jour*"?[17] There are so many other oppressed and repressed groups! Why did I choose LGBT blacks and Latinas/os as an example to justify a change in the driving question of theological anthropology?

1. LGBT blacks and Latinas/os are being denied equality in society and church exclusively because of their sexual orientation. LGBT Latinas/os and blacks are the victims of a frightening numbers of violent hate crimes and of an even higher number of cases of harassment.

LGBT blacks and Latinas/os have to deal with the prejudices and racism of the dominant, because they are black and Latina/o; and we, black and Latina/o theologians, have spoken eloquently and passionately on what these prejudices and racism mean. But LGBT Latinos/as and blacks *also* have to deal with the prejudices and persecution inflicted on them because of their sexual orientation—prejudices and persecution coming not only from the dominant European Americans but also, and morally worse, from other blacks and Latinos/as. Yet on this added oppression, unfortunately, most of us have been unexplainably silent. Are our sins less sinful than those committed by European Americans?

Arguments are used to justify the denial of equality and the passing of legislation to repress and suppress the presence and human rights of LGBT persons in society and church. Worse, however, is that many of these arguments and support for the legislation, and the denial of LGBTs' rights as human beings, come from within our families, our neighborhoods, our communities, and our churches. The outsider is not the sole oppressor here. We, Latinas/os and blacks, are too, and against our own.[18]

2. If we look at the biblical record, there is little that contemporary exegesis could allow us to claim as condemnatory of homosexuality as it is understood today.[19] The use of a handful of biblical texts[20] to justify the condemnation or repression of LGBT persons should remind us, however, of the use of biblical texts in order to justify black slavery, the colonial and postcolonial genocide of Amerindian natives, and so many other social horrors; otherwise good Christians felt justified, and most theological voices of the time concurred in this unfortunate use of the Scriptures.[21]

Philosophy, theology, the sciences, and the Bible for centuries agreed with and justified the "natural" character of slavery.[22] Scientists, theologians, philosophers, and Bible readers shielded themselves behind the scientific or religious arguments that they had created in order to wash their hands of ethical responsibilities. They, the beneficiaries of slavery and of so many other injustices, created the arguments that justified their benefits because oppression was, according to their best theories, perfectly natural, a mandate of natural law, and even willed by God. They asked themselves, How could a God-fearing and right-thinking person stand against such evidence? Should it surprise us, then, that the first universal and unequivocal condemnation of slavery within the Catholic Church came in 1965, in a document of the Second Vatican Council?[23]

I readily admit that present-day violence against LGBT persons is not equal to slavery, and I am not suggesting such parity; and I unequivocally admit that LGBT persons are not the only victims of social prejudices.[24] I am saying, however, that we already know the horrors that arguments based on biblical or natural evidence, or on what passed unchallenged for "evidence," inflicted on millions of other human beings. And now that similarly constructed evidence is being used to inflict serious suffering on others very publicly, including LGBT persons, we black and Latina/o theologians cannot remain silent or pretend that we do not hear or see. We who have raised our voices against domestic violence and racism, against all forms of discrimination and injustices, cannot call for a "rain check" in relation to the millions of LGBTs, and especially black and Latina/o LGBTs, who suffer renewed persecution, harassment, and violence; silence or absence regarding these *human rights* issues is neither morally acceptable nor speaks well of the credibility of our theologies. We cannot morally pass by the pretended biblical and natural theological arguments that justify discrimination and injustice against humans in the name of God.

3. Another reason for choosing LGBT blacks and Latinas/os as an example of our silences and absences, and to justify a change in the driving question of theological anthropology is that *humanitas* is the dynamic, living intersection of our real-life and diverse contextualizations. I said earlier that *humanitas* does not exist, and has never existed, as a generic nature, but as the living intersection of specific, diverse contextualizations that recognize one another as human precisely because they recognize in one another the historical reality of unfolding, specific, and diverse contextualizations. And so I ask, Do we, black and Latina/o Catholic theologians, not recognize in LGBT Latinas/os and blacks an evident set of historically unfolding, living, specific, and diverse contextualizations? In other words, should we not be ethically required in our theologies to state clearly that LGBT persons are evidently identifiable as human, and therefore cannot be denied *any* human or civil right?[25] Should we not be required to insist on this, given the current and very public debate concerning the human and civil rights of LGBT persons in U.S. society?

LGBT persons evidence and are the intersections of specific, living, historical, and diverse contextualizations. They are gendered, raced, sexually oriented, classed, socially positioned, and so forth, just as everyone else. These contextualizations are not separable among LGBT persons any more than they could be among others. Humans *are* the living intersection and not the mere theoretical listing of contextualizations. Humans *are* the historical and existential unfolding of the intersection and not the mere juxtaposition of contextualizations. And, therefore, LGBT persons could not be human persons if they somehow bracketed or dismissed their sexual orientation; their *humanitas* is dependent on their also being sexually oriented, just as everyone else. To be really human requires the recognition and acceptance of one's sexual orientation, and this applies equally to heterosexuals as to LGBT persons. And so, to ask Who are human persons? necessarily includes (in the question and in the answer) the explicit recognition and acceptance of human sexual orientations.

We, Latina/o and black Catholic theologians, have not hesitated to remind ourselves and the theological academy that race, gender, ethnicity, and culture (and poverty, social location, etc.) cannot be overlooked or played down in theology if professional theology and theologians intend to address real-life situations and issues in the name of the Christian gospel. Therefore, and for exactly the same reasons, we now cannot ignore LGBT blacks and Latinas/os in our theologies, because sexual orientation is an unavoidable real contextualization—as real and unavoidable as race, gender, ethnicity, or culture. Heterosexuality is no more normative than whiteness, maleness, or Eurocentrism. We have always, and rightly, insisted that dominance is not an ethically or theologically acceptable argument for the exclusion of the nondominant, and now we must apply that same argument to ourselves in reference to our own black and Latina/o LGBT sisters and brothers.[26]

As the driving question for theological anthropology, Who are human persons? will not allow us to make exceptions among humans. It will, on the contrary, make us deal with issues of power, prejudices, and manipulation of truth; and it will force us to admit the potential use of ourselves and of our scholarship in support of the dominant.

Which is worse, to die from stabbing with a knife or from stabbing with a dagger? We could theorize an answer; but if we asked the victims of stabbing, they would probably consider our theorizing irrelevant if not obscene. Which, then, is worse, to suffer prejudice and persecution because of the color of one's skin, or because of one's ethnicity, or because of one's gender, or because of one's social class, or because of one's political options, or because of one's sexual orientation? If we asked the victims of prejudice and persecution, they too would probably think our theorizing irrelevant and probably obscene. We cannot morally descend to the level of making the victims compete with one another, as if in a Roman circus, for the entertainment of the dominant and the intellectual curiosity of the scholarly. Unfortunately, sometimes blacks and Latinas/os have tried to impose on themselves the roles of competing victims, forgetful of who really benefits from such demeaning roles.

4. What makes blacks and/or Latinas/os *human* persons is not only, or even mainly, race or ethnicity. We are Latinas/os or black because of our gender, our social class, our communities' history, *and* our sexual orientation (and other intersecting contextualizations). We cannot be human without the intersection of all of them. Even if when theorizing we might wish to focus on one or another contextualization, in real life we cannot choose. In real life, our self-disclosing identity is complex; and, as I have stated already, we *are* the living intersection of various contextualizations. In real life we cannot pick one as more relevant or determining than the others.

If a Latina or a black woman cannot be Latina or black without her gender, the same must be said of Latino and black men. But gender is not just biological, it is cultural too; and that is why our respective communities suffer still from gender bias, domestic violence, and other very real consequences of the specific, living, historical intersections of cultural maleness and cultural womanness among our peoples. The same can and must be said of sexual orientation. It is not just biological, but also cultural; and it impacts identity as much and in similar, even if distinguishable, ways as social class, race, ethnicity, and gender do.

A renewed theological anthropology cannot avoid reflecting on the complexity and diversity of intersecting contextualizations. Each is as defining of *humanitas* as the other, and jointly they are self-disclosing of identities. We are human *at and as* the specific, living, historical intersection of varied contextualizations.

Theological anthropology, of course, should it choose to continue with its earlier, typical driving question, What is the human person?, will not be able to escape the hegemonic requirement to prioritize contextualizations[27] and perhaps dismiss some in order to fit a preconceived notion of *humanitas* that resembles more the imperial paradigm of the dominant[28] than the reality of the real human world. I hope that black and Latina/o Catholic theologians will not allow themselves to be seduced into this trap.

There is no conclusion to this paper—perhaps there can be no conclusion. My purpose was to raise some questions regarding theological anthropology and, perhaps more uncomfortably, to ask why our theologies have been absent and silent from one of the more important civil- and human-rights struggles of our day. I hope to have raised the questions and made us feel sufficiently uncomfortable to provoke our reflection and engagement. If we Latina/o and black Catholic theologians disclose who we are, we will inevitably see our sexual orientations as determining our identities and our shared *humanitas* as much as race, culture, and gender are. It is perhaps time to admit the complexity of our respective and shared identities and move beyond the insufficient, and ultimately sterile, descriptions of one another mostly in terms of only three contextualizations: race, culture, and gender.[29]

Appendix:
Some National Statistics on LGBT Latinas/os and Blacks (June 2006)

Note 1. Where no specific reference is made to black or Latina/o LGBTs, it should be assumed that the data reflect the general statistics reported for LGBTs in U.S. society. And where no specific reference is made to the general black and/or Latina/o populations, it should be assumed that there they generally reflect the statistical data reported for the overall U.S. population.

Note 2. All statistics below were taken from different printed and Internet sources (all acknowledged herein). All sources were checked for their history of credibility and sound data gathering. There is no claim made herein, however, that the data below are definitive. There are margins of error, and the statistics are methodologically adequate approximations to reality.

Note 3. All statistics below were gathered for the exclusive purpose of providing substantiation to the present paper. Statistics were gathered, therefore, in view of this paper's needs and theoretical argument. No attempt was made to be statistically or demographically exhaustive or to cover all issues related to black and Latina/o LGBT persons in the United States. The argument of the present paper did not require such comprehensiveness.

Note 4. When attempting to describe or understand black and Latina/o LGBT persons it is necessary to consider that they suffer the consequences of homophobia, hate crimes, and so forth, just as the broader U.S. LGBT population does. They likewise suffer from the homophobia and rejection more typical of their respective black or Latina/o communities, while also suffering the consequences of racism and ethnic prejudice against blacks and Latinas/os in the United States. Black and Latina/o LGBT persons, therefore, live under three distinguishable but historically inseparable layers of anti-LGBT prejudice, harassment, and violence.

How Many U.S. Blacks and Latina/os Are LGBT?

According to the U.S. Census Bureau (2005), 13 percent of the overall U.S. population is black, and 14 percent of the overall U.S. population is Latina/o.

- It is somewhat surprising that the U.S. Census Bureau also reports that 47.9 percent of all Latinas/os further describe themselves as white and the remaining 52.1 percent describe themselves as "mixed race" or "other."

About 10 percent of the overall U.S. population can be identified as LGBT. But note the following:

- Any valid statistical data on the percentage of LGBTs in the general population depends on self-disclosure to researchers. Consequently, given ambient homophobia and real danger of hate crimes, it can be argued that in some regions and contexts there occurs an almost inevitable undercounting.
- Furthermore, given the real social consequences and social stresses involved in self-disclosure as LGBT, it must be assumed that undercounting (and clearly not the opposite) would impact the accuracy of the statistical data. (See below for data on hate crimes, violence, harassment, etc.)

It is also possible to work with a figure of 10 percent gay and bisexual men in the overall U.S. male population, even when correcting the methodology, samples, and resulting data from the Kinsey Reports (see A. C. Kinsey et al., *Sexual Behavior in the Human Male* [Philadelphia: W. B. Saunders, 1948]; and idem, *Sexual Behavior in the Human Female* [Philadelphia: W. B. Saunders, 1953]).

- C. Bagley and P. Tremblay give a figure, correcting Kinsey, of approximately 15 percent gay and bisexual men (see

"On the Prevalence of Homosexuality and Bisexuality in a Random Community Survey of 750 Men Aged 18 to 27," *Journal of Homosexuality* 36, no. 2 [1998]: 1-18).

- T. W. Smith reports 5 percent gay and bisexual men, also correcting Kinsey (see "American Sexual Behavior: Trends, Socio-Demographic Differences, and Risk Behavior," at http://www.norc.uchicago.edu/issues/ [University of Chicago, National Opinion Research Center, 2003]).

- R. Hawkins et al. also report 10 percent gays and bisexuals (among men and women), even after correcting and updating the Kinsey scale (see "Homoerotic, Homosexual, and Ambisexual Behavior," at http://www2.hu-berlin .de/sexology/IES/xmain.html [*International Encyclopedia of Sexuality,* ed. R. T. Francoeur, vols. I-IV (1997-2001)]).

- Consequently, if the percentage of LGBT in the general population (among men, but probably also among women) is somewhere between 5 and 15 percent, then the 10 percent figure remains reasonably adequate (if not completely accurate, given what was stated earlier about undercounting and the effects and pressures of self-disclosure).

About 10 percent of the black and Latina/o populations in the United States are LGBT, with geographical variations (as for the percentage of homosexual persons in the general population) (see R. Hawkins et al., "Homoerotic, Homosexual, and Ambisexual Behavior"). Evidently, the 10 percent figure is dependent on self-disclosure of blacks and Latinas/os to researchers.

- The percentages of black or Latina/o LGBTs vary geographically across the United States. For example, in San Diego there are about 6 percent LBGT blacks within the overall local black population (less than the national average), but there are about 27 percent LGBT Latinas/os within the overall local Latina/o population (more than double the national average). Source: 2000 U.S. Census GSS figures projected to 2005.

- Hawkins et al. ("Homoerotic, Homosexual, and Ambisexual Behavior") report that U.S. blacks and Latinas/os (for a variety of cultural reasons) are less tolerant of LGBTs than European Americans are.

Living as an LGBT Person in the United States

The statistics in this section are not exhaustive or complete. They are intended only for the purpose of presenting a broad picture and emphasizing some stresses and difficulties. They reflect data applicable to the overall LGBT population in the United States, but they are also applicable *mutatis mutandi* to black and Latina/o LGBTs.

Depending on geographic location in the United States, anywhere from 52 to 87 percent of all LGBT persons report having experienced verbal or physical harassment more than once in any given year (Case Western Reserve University study, 2004). Every year nearly half a million LGBT persons suffer violence (domestic, hate crimes, etc.) because of their sexual orientation (University of Wisconsin study, 2003).

According to the National Coalition of Anti-Violence Programs (2003, compared to 2002), in only one year, reported violent crimes against LGBT persons because of their sexual orientation dramatically increased across the United States. Examples include the following:

- in Chicago, violent crimes against LGBTs went up 120 percent
- in New York City, violent crimes against LGBTs went up 43 percent
- in San Francisco, violent crime against LGBTs went up 14 percent
- in the state of Connecticut, violent crimes against LGBTs went up 450 percent
- in the state of Colorado, violent crimes against LGBTs went up 133 percent

It seems that LGBT youth are more vulnerable and the more frequent victims of crimes against LGBTs. Examples include the following:

- 28 percent of all LGBT youth drop out of school because of harassment (Case Western Reserve University study, 2004)
- 26 percent of LGBT teens were forced into homelessness by their own families because of the teens' sexual orientation (Safe Schools Coalition, 2005)
- 35 percent of all homeless teens in the United States are LGBT (Safe Schools Coalition, 2005)

In reference to LGBT youth, the American Civil Liberties Union reported the following statistics in 2005:

- 84 percent of all LGBT youth reported (in 2001) being the object of frequent homophobic statements in schools, neighborhoods, etc.
- 81 percent of all LGBT youth reported that, in their schools, no teacher or administrator ever came to their defense or attempted to do anything to stop homophobic slurs on campus
- 69 percent of all LGBT youth reported serious verbal harassment in school
- 65 percent of all LGBT youth reported serious sexual harassment in school
- 42 percent of all LGBT youth reported physical harassment in school or neighborhood
- 21 percent of all LGBT youth reported being the victims of physical violence in school, home, or neighborhood because of their perceived sexual orientation
- 90 percent of transgender youth felt physically threatened in school, home, or neighborhood.
- approximately three times as many LGBT youth commit suicide as heterosexual youth (also reported as far back as 1989 by the U.S. Department of Education)

The Human Rights Campaign reported in 2005 that in thirty-four states a person can be legally fired from his/her job for being lesbian, gay, or bisexual; a transgender person can legally lose his/her employment (for being transgender) in forty-four states.

Nationally, gay and bisexual men (or men perceived to be gay or bisexual) earned 25 percent less than men perceived to be heterosexual. But no similar find was reported in reference to lesbians (A. K. Baumle, D. Compton, and D. L. Poston, *The Social Demography of Sexual Orientation* [New York: SUNY Press, forthcoming], chapter 7).

It must be understood, however, that all of the above statistics on the general U.S. population or on the general U.S. LGBT population are also applicable to blacks and Latinas/os, but with the following aggravating factors:

- Black and Latina/o LGBT persons, *because* they are black and Latina/o in the United States, *also* suffer under the same burdens of racism, ethnic prejudices, income differences, hate crimes, etc., as the overall U.S. black and Latina/o populations. Some of the racism and prejudice that black and Latina/o LGBTs have to deal with comes from white LGBT persons.
- Black and Latina/o LGBT persons, *also* suffer the intolerance, prejudices, etc., that specifically reflect the biases and dynamics of the overall black and Latina/o populations in addition to suffering, as all LGBTs, at the hands of ambient homophobia and other prejudices and crimes against LGBTs.

To Complicate Black and Latina/o LGBT Reality Further: Living with HIV/AIDS (Source: Centers for Disease Control, 2005, and Kaiser Family Foundation, 2005)

Latinas/os are 20 percent and blacks are 39 percent of all diagnosed cases of persons living with HIV/AIDS in the United States.

Together, therefore, blacks and Latinas/os are 59 percent of all persons in the United States living with HIV/AIDS, yet they represent only 27 percent of the total population of the country.

In 2001, HIV/AIDS was the third leading cause of death among U.S. Latino men and the fourth leading cause of death among U.S. Latina women.

Most Latinas/os living with HIV/AIDS also live in poverty. Note the following examples:

- 47 percent of all Mexican or Mexican American persons living with HIV/AIDS in the United States also live in poverty
- 59 percent of all Puerto Rican persons living with HIV/AIDS in the United States also live in poverty
- although we could not find reliable figures on poverty among blacks living with HIV/AIDS, it can be reasonably assumed that most blacks living with HIV/AIDS also live in poverty, because approximately 45 percent of blacks living with HIV/AIDS rely on public insurance or Medicaid for health care and treatment

Of all black men living with HIV/AIDS in the United States, 32 percent are gay or bisexual. Of all black women living with HIV/AIDS in the United States, only 1 percent are lesbians or bisexual. No reliable figures could be found for black transgender persons.

Of all Latino men living with HIV/AIDS in the United States, 66 percent are gay or bisexual. Of all Latina women living with HIV/AIDS in the United States, only 3 percent are lesbians or bisexual. No reliable figures could be found for Latina/o transgender persons.

Notes

1. For a synthetic and good panoramic presentation of theological anthropology throughout the twentieth century, see P. Watté, "Antropología

teológica y hamartiología en el siglo XX," in *La teología en el siglo XX,* ed. H. Vorgrimler and R. vander Gucht (Madrid: Biblioteca de Autores Cristianos, 1974), 3:47-62. There have been some important exceptions to the panorama I just painted, however. One such important exception is the theological anthropology of Karl Rahner, which he so intimately connected with (and derived from) Christology. See, for example, "Reflexiones teológicas sobre la antropología y la protología," in *Mysterium Salutis: Manual de teología como historia de la salvación,* ed. J. Feiner and M. Löhrer, 2d ed. (Madrid: Ediciones Cristiandad, 1977), 2:341-52. Nevertheless, the same Rahner who wrote in *Mysterium Salutis* also wrote the lengthy entry on theological anthropology (still asking "What is the human person?") in the widely read and very influential *Sacramentum Mundi* (see *Sacramentum Mundi: Enciclopedia teológica,* ed. K. Rahner, vols. I-VI [Barcelona: Editorial Herder, 1976]). Rahner's article on theological anthropology is in 1:286-96. The typical driving question of theological anthropology is also frequently found in other influential European theological dictionaries of post–Vatican II theology (often translated into many other languages). For example, G. Barbaglio and S. Dianich, eds., *Nuevo diccionario de teología,* vols. I and II (Madrid: Ediciones Cristiandad, 1982); and L. Pacomio et al., eds., *Dizionario teologico interdisciplinare,* vols. I-IV (Genoa: Marietti Editori, 1977). See also A. O. Dyson, "Anthropology, Christian," in *The Westminster Dictionary of Christian Theology,* ed. A. Richardson and J. Bowden (Philadelphia: Westminster Press, 1983), 23-26; and M. Scanlon, "Anthropology, Christian," in *New Dictionary of Theology,* ed. J. Komonchak, M. Collins, and D. Lane (Wilmington, Del.: Michael Glazier, 1987), 27-41.

2. I must again emphasize that both of these questions, in theological anthropology, are *theological.* Therefore, both of them will necessarily seek answers ("generic" or "real," to use my characterizations) that attempt to discover the connections between (at least) humanness (and humans) and God, Christ, grace, revelation, and faith. Hence, even if in different ways, all theological anthropologies can agree with M. Scanlon's assertion that "personhood describes an anthropology whose roots are in the religious soil of the bible" ("Anthropology, Christian," in *New Dictionary of Theology,* 27-41). While our two questions (i.e., What is the human person? and Who are human persons?") remain "in the religious soil of the bible," they still reflect distinct and very different approaches to theological anthropology.

3. See, again, R. Watté's article in *La teología en el siglo XX* (n. 1, above). Also see A. O. Graff, *In the Embrace of God: Feminist Approaches to Theological Anthropology* (Eugene, Ore.: Wipf & Stock, 2005). J. I. González Faus

proposed a reformed theological anthropology in his *Proyecto de hermano: Visión creyente del hombre* (Santander: Editorial Sal Terrae, 1987), but what this author achieved in some areas in this masterful book might have been compromised by his lack of awareness of other equally crucial areas (certainly for a book published in 1987). Gender, ethnicity, and race, for example, do not seem important to González Faus's theological anthropology. M. H. Díaz attempts a creative balance between the two questions in his *On Being Human: U.S. Hispanic and Rahnerian Perspectives* (Maryknoll, N.Y.: Orbis Books, 2001) but decidedly prioritizes "*Who* is a human person?" in his "*Dime con quién andas y te diré quién eres*: We Walk-with Our Lady of Charity," in *From the Heart of Our People: Latino/a Explorations in Catholic Systematic Theology,* ed. O. O. Espín and M. H. Díaz (Maryknoll, N.Y.: Orbis Books, 1999), 153-71.

4. I have difficulty with the idea of a *humanum* as an underlying quality, substratum, essence, or nature that distinguishes us as human. *Humanum* does not refer to any historical, contextualized persons and communities. Its supposed universality exists strictly and exclusively in the realm of (mostly Western) theory. Furthermore, *humanum,* given its undeniable essentialist presuppositions, raises other serious questions. The proposed understanding of *humanitas* herein tries to avoid these concerns and essentialist presuppositions.

5. An intercultural perspective (e.g., as that elaborated by the philosopher Raúl Fornet-Betancourt) might resolve the interesting objections (was it an impasse?) raised by both James Nickoloff and Carmen Nanko-Fernández in their respective papers on identity, which were presented at the sixtieth annual convention (2005) of the Catholic Theological Society of America. See G. Riebe-Estrella, "Latina/o Theology: Diversity, Hybridity, and Commonality," in *Proceedings of the Sixtieth Annual Convention, Catholic Theological Society of America* (2005), 142-43. On this, see also the remarkably insightful (and very much ahead of his time) Máximo Castro Turbiano, *Estudios filosóficos* (Havana: Sociedad Cubana de Filosofía, 1954), 54-83.

6. All contextualizations and their intersections are historical human constructs. Even gender and sexual orientation, clearly grounded in biology, are not experienced by humans *merely* as biological but *emphatically* as cultural. And because they are experienced as cultural, then they are also experienced as ethical. The same must be said of skin color (even when recognizing that skin color is not coextensive with race).

7. Not in contradiction to what I just stated, but perhaps as expansion and further clarification, it might be important to consider M. P. Aquino's

assertion that (when reflecting on human identities and, thus, on human differences) "the central problem is not the value adjudicated to human differences but the political use of them that leaves intact a kyriarchical paradigm of globalization" ("Theology and Identity in the Context of Globalization," in *The Oxford Handbook of Feminist Theology,* ed. S. Briggs and M. McClintock Fulkerson [Oxford: Oxford University Press, forthcoming]). A parallel reflection by the same author is "Teología crítica y dogmatismos religiosos: Desafíos y propuestas," in *Teologia e sociedade: Relevância e funções,* ed. Sociedade de Teologia e Ciências da Religião (São Paulo: Edições Paulinas, forthcoming).

8. The validity and legitimacy of a theory (theological and otherwise) do not rest exclusively with its ability to describe or analyze. Necessary too (and this is especially so for theology) are a theory's *ethical* purpose and use. Who benefits from a theory? and Whose interests are reflected in a theory? are, in my estimation, indispensable questions to raise when confronted with any theory, just as important as the theory's claim to analytical or descriptive competence. It would be the combination of competence *and* ethics (at least) that validates and legitimizes a theory. Without the ethical evaluation of its purpose and use, a theory might, in real life, be only an ideologically manipulative (and manipulated) theoretical artifact. For a further expansion on this, see A. Gramsci, *Os intelectuais ea organização da cultura,* 3rd ed. (Rio de Janeiro: Editora Civilização Brasileira, 1979). Latina/o theologians, almost two decades ago, spent many hours discussing the key criteria for the validation, and the identity of the validators, of Latina/o theology. It might be wise to return to and to move forward some of those discussions, because they would remind us that real persons and real communities are necessary (though not the exclusive) validators of our theology; and the interests, reality, and faith of real persons and communities are indispensable criteria of validation (although, again, not the exclusive criteria).

9. The historically typical driving question in theological anthropology (What is the human person?) cannot, of course, be held solely responsible for justifying the horrors inflicted by European Christians on Amerindians and Africans in the sixteenth century, just as theological anthropology cannot bear the exclusive blame for subsequent centuries of oppression and slavery. But theological anthropology is not blameless either; it bears a heavy ideological responsibility for justifying in the name of God much of what historically happened and for what continues to happen to millions of people. Sixteenth-century theologians knew the difference between the two anthropological questions and the consequences of asking each, as illustrated by

the Las Casas-Sepúlveda controversy of the 1550s. Already in 1511, Montesinos preached the difference. But it seems that most theologians of the time preferred the benefits and respectability they received from the dominant and not from defending justice. Acceptance by the powerful (in academy, society, and church) seems to have been the great temptation for theologians who engaged the key anthropological questions. The cost of respectability was ethical blindness, and the *real* consequence (besides the damage inflicted on theology and ethics) was the extraordinary and prolonged suffering of millions of human beings.

10. See Luke 7:36-50 and Luke 10:29-37.

11. This sermon and other texts can be found in F. Jay, ed., *Three Dominican Pioneers in the New World: Antonio de Montesinos, Domingo de Betanzos, Gonzalo Lucero* (Lewiston, N.Y.: Edwin Mellen, 2002).

12. The sermons and a number of other texts by Jaca and Moiráns are in: J. T. López García, ed., *Dos defensores de los esclavos negros en el siglo XVII* (Caracas: Editorial Arte, 1982). See also J. A. Carreras, *Esclavitud, abolición y racismo* (Havana: Editorial de Ciencias Sociales, 1985).

13. As we know from history, these three friars were certainly not the only ones to raise their voices, at considerable personal risk, in the name of justice and the gospel. The list of Christian defenders of the rights of the oppressed in the Americas is very long and distinguished. Nevertheless, we must admit that these great Christians (from Antonio de Montesinos to César Chávez, and from Francisco José de Jaca to Martin Luther King) are remembered not just because of their admirable courage but because they were the exceptions. They stood out in their respective historical moments precisely because most others did not.

14. An exception was one session within the ACHTUS colloquium held in Washington, D.C., a few years ago. And yet, this was barely one session within one colloquium out of eighteen ACHTUS annual colloquia (to 2006), consisting of four long sessions each. Although we applaud the theologians C. Nanko Fernández and J. Nickoloff, who opened the discussion at that ACHTUS colloquium, the point I am making here remains: the discussion in Washington has had no further consequences in our theologies.

15. See Jay, ed., *Three Dominican Pioneers in the New World* (n. 11).

16. See the appendix for statistics on violence and other hate crimes against LGBT persons.

17. For a general statistical overview of the black and Latina/o LGBT populations, and some of the prejudices and violence they live under in the United States, see the appendix at the end of the present article.

18. Although Hans Urs von Balthasar did not engage in any discussion of LGBT rights, I do recall his writing that many of today's theologians, deaf to the cries of their fellow humans, could be accused of cowardly passing by our world's anguish and pain. Detached from the real present, they continue to develop their theologies. Von Balthasar's phrase, much harsher in the original, is in *The Christian and Anxiety* (San Francisco: Ignatius Press, 2000), 27.

19. From among the vast literature, see R. Scroggs, *The New Testament and Homosexuality* (Philadelphia: Fortress Press, 1983); J. Boswell, *Christianity, Social Tolerance and Homosexuality* (Chicago: University of Chicago Press, 1980); and J. Miner and J. T. Connoley, *The Children Are Free: Re-examining the Biblical Evidence on Same-Sex Relationships* (Indianapolis: Jesus Metropolitan Community Church, 2002).

20. And these texts are a handful indeed, especially when compared with the myriad biblical commands to love the poor, to defend the oppressed and immigrant, and to act compassionately toward all. It appears to border on the hypocritical when the same persons and communities that argue against the dignity and rights of LGBT persons on biblical grounds become conveniently absent and silent in the struggles for justice of the oppressed and the immigrant, as clearly and repeatedly mandated by hundreds of biblical texts.

21. See J. M. Lima Lira, *A evangelização do negro no período colonial brasileiro* (São Paulo: Edições Loyola, 1983); J. Andrés-Gallegos and J. M. García Añoveros, *La Iglesia y la esclavitud de los negros* (Pamplona: Ediciones de la Universidad de Navarra, 2002); J. F. Maxwell, *Slavery and the Catholic Church* (London: Barry Rose Publishers, 1975); M. Moreno Fraginals, *La historia como arma, y otros estudios sobre esclavos, ingenios y plantaciones* (Barcelona: Editorial Crítica, 1983); L. Rivera Pagán, *Evangelización y violencia: La conquista de América* (San Juan: Editorial Cemí, 1991).

22. I am not bringing up slavery in this paper because we are engaged in a dialogue with our black Catholic colleagues. Evidently, slavery is historically very important for them too. I refer to slavery here because we Latinas/os must begin to recognize the presence of Africa and her descendants in our own communities—not as demographic oddities but as a significant (numerically, historically, and culturally) part of the racial and cultural mix that historically gave birth to our communities. We Latinas/os are as racially and culturally *mulatas/os* as we are *mestizas/os*. In other words, slavery and its horrors are also part of *our* Latina/o history too. A recent and excellent *theological* contribution to this issue is Michelle González, *Afro-Cuban Theology* (Gainesville: University Press of Florida, 2006). See also O. Espín, ed., *Born from Slaves and Criollos/as: Towards a Cuban-American Inter-Religious Dia-*

logue (Maryknoll, N.Y.: Orbis Books, forthcoming 2008); and idem, *Evangelización y religiones negras,* vols. I-IV (Rio de Janeiro: Ed. PUC, 1984). From the perspective of history and the various social sciences, the bibliography on the presence of Africa and descendants from Africa in Latin America and among U.S. Latinas/os is truly immense. Cuban Americans might do well to read Rafael Fermoselle's *Política y color en Cuba* (Montevideo: Ediciones Géminis, 1974) for a different interpretation of the role of slaves, slavery, and race in Cuba's process of independence and in the country's early republican history.

23. See *Gaudium et Spes*, nn. 27, 29, 41. See also J. F. Maxwell, *Slavery and the Catholic Church* (n. 21, above). The 1992 *Catechism of the Catholic Church* (n. 2414) is the first worldwide Catholic *catechetical* document that explicitly condemns the system and practice of slavery as sinful, against God's will, and a violation of human dignity.

24. It is impossible today in the United States, for example, to avoid being confronted with nearly hysterical anti-immigrant posturing—even by members of racial and ethnic minorities and not solely by the dominant white. Couched sometimes in the language of national security or of concerns about employment and budgets, the obvious (some might say blatant) motivations are most frequently racist, religious (i.e., anti-Catholic, anti-Muslim), and xenophobic. As Cardinal R. Mahoney (of Los Angeles) has recently reminded us (March 2006), the Catholic Church must not yield to such hysteria and must be willing to risk confrontation with the government in order to clearly and without ambivalence stand with and for the rights of immigrants (*because* immigrants are human persons with God-given dignity and inalienable rights, *regardless of any and every other concern*, and *because* the church, in the exercise of its mission of compassion and justice, must not yield to the pressures of the dominant). Immigration and immigrants, I might add, could very well qualify as another silence and absence in black and Latina/o Catholic theologies. The spring 2006 mass mobilizations in the United States in favor of immigrants (especially of the undocumented) are a sign that Latino/a and black theologians must soon theologically deal with immigration and the rights of the undocumented as a human rights issue (and hence, as a crucial issue for a *Catholic* theological anthropology). Unfortunately, the list of other victims of U.S. social prejudice remains very long.

25. *Gaudium et Spes* could not have been clearer: "Any kind of social or cultural discrimination in basic personal rights on the grounds of sex, race, color, social condition, language or religion, must be curbed and eradicated

as incompatible with God's design" (n. 29). And in order to leave no doubt, the same conciliar document (n. 26) further states: "[All persons] ought, therefore, to have ready access to *all* that is necessary for living a genuinely human life: for example, food, clothing, housing, the right to freely choose their state of life and set up a family, the right to education, work, to their good name, to respect, to proper knowledge, the right to act according to the dictates of conscience and to safeguard their privacy, and rightful freedom, including freedom of religion." If these are the inalienable rights of *all* persons, it is obvious (and logically necessary) that these *too* are the inalienable rights of all LGBT persons.

26. The U.S. Catholic bishops' statement *Always Our Children: A Pastoral Message to Parents of Homosexual Children and Suggestions for Pastoral Ministers* (1997), itself restating and corroborating the teaching of an earlier pastoral document, clearly and explicitly says (in part IV): "The teachings of the Church make it clear that the fundamental human rights of homosexual persons must be defended and that all of us must strive to eliminate any forms of injustice, oppression, or violence against them (cf. *The Pastoral Care of Homosexual Persons*, 1986, no. 10)."

27. But according to whose criteria? And why? And for whose benefit?

28. Probably and conveniently referred to as a "universally present" and "universally valid" *humanum.*

29. For a significant number of black and Latina/o Catholic theologians, race and culture remain the two central and most crucial contextualizations to discuss when considering identity. Gender (as part of the discussion on black and/or Latina/o identity), unfortunately, remains for some that which sexual orientation is still for most.

3

Contours of a Latino/a
Theology of Religions

In Dialogue with the Lukumí Religion

Most contemporary Catholic theologies of religions refer to religious universes that have little to do with the experience of the
majority of Catholics, since most Catholics in the world today are
of Latin American descent.[1] In the United States, where nearly half
of all Catholics are Latino/a,[2] theologies of religion have not been
engaged by Latino/a theologians or by Latino/a Catholics[3] in general, mostly because theologies of religions have usually seemed to
us so foreign and not urgent. And yet, oddly enough, U.S. Latino/a
theology has also not reflected in any significant and sustained
manner on those non-Christian religions that live within the
Latino/a cultural world.[4] The non-Christian religions present
among U.S. Latinos/as are either religions that survive from the
native populations of this continent or African religions brought to
the Americas by the millions of women and men enslaved during
the colonial period.

Obviously, neither native nor African religions exist today
among Latin Americans or among U.S. Latinos/as as they were

An earlier version of this paper was presented at the 2004 convention of the Catholic Theological Society of America, in Reston, Virginia. I am very grateful to Prof. Francis Clooney for
the invitation, and to him and Prof. Nancy Pineda-Madrid for their valuable and thoughtful
responses at the CTSA convention.

before the arrival of the Europeans or before the slave trade. Both native and African religious universes have been deeply impacted by their encounter with Catholicism and with European cultures. And yet, in spite of the horrors of slavery, of conquest, of genocide, of racist laws, and of many misguided attempts at evangelization, both religious universes have managed to survive. In the case of the African religions, they have also managed to thrive on our side of the Atlantic.

In this article I want to present a broad silhouette of what a U.S. Latino/a theology of religions might be like, in dialogue with the main non-Christian religion in our own Latino/a cultural backyard.[5] I realize that this theology is yet to be constructed, but at this time and in this brief paper, I can do no more than paint a very broad picture with equally broad strokes in an attempt to *suggest* elements, components, sources, and attitudes needed for a Latino/a theology of religions, while avoiding the temptation to present such a theology.

I will begin by addressing what I think are, or should be, the general assumptions for a Latino/a theology of religions and then proceed to see how these might play when placed in dialogue with the Lukumí religion of Yoruba roots, which is arguably the largest of the non-Christian religions in the Latin American and U.S. Latino/a contexts.[6]

Assumptions and Sources
for a Latino/a Theology of Religions

What Do We Mean by "Theology of Religions"?
What Are Its Assumptions?

Any theology of religions, in my view, is first and foremost a Christian reflection on the meaning and actions of God's grace in human societies, in human religions, and in human persons. Any theology of religions is a Christian construct that attempts to understand the love of God, the providence of God, and the grace of God at work in non-Christian contexts; and thus, any theology of religions is ultimately for the benefit of Christian self-understanding. Put briefly, a theology of religions is a consequence of, and a contribution to, *Christian* soteriology, theological anthropology, and spirituality.[7]

Consequently, the main and nonnegotiable assumption in any Catholic theology of religions is that God, as understood in mainstream Christian tradition, is loving, merciful, and compassionate toward all human beings, regardless of any moral, racial, sexual, social, religious, or cultural condition. God, as understood by mainstream Christian tradition, is loving and compassionate to all human beings, always and everywhere, without limits, without conditions, and without exceptions.

This nonnegotiable assumption about God is what brings Christians to reflect on how God expresses God's merciful and loving compassion to and among non-Christians (note, please, that it is "how," not "whether"). This assumption requires the corollary that God, in fact, loves and shows merciful compassion to and among non-Christians, and therefore that divine grace acts in, through, and for them too. This leads to a third required assumption: namely, that non-Christians can and do experience God's love and grace, even if they might not name, know, or explain it in a Christian manner.

Because religions play such a significant role in shaping human societies, cultures, and persons—specifically shaping social and individual identities—the study of religions as loci of God's grace-filled action is a worthy, important, and much-needed theological task. This task, however, should not be a justification for Christian imperialism, or sense of superiority, or racism;[8] and it certainly cannot be a legitimation of theological constructs that attempt to "tell" God where, how, and for whom divine grace should act. God is absolute, and so is God's grace. This absoluteness, and the mystery and gratuity it implies, cannot be curtailed by theology or church doctrine; nor can theology or doctrine pre-

tend to have the final explanation of God's mystery and gratu-
itous grace. Any such attempt would bear the stench of cultural or
ecclesial idolatry.

A theology of religions honestly acknowledging humankind's
religious and cultural diversity is ultimately about God's mystery,
God's grace, and God's unfathomable compassion toward
humankind, while holding fast to that magnificent intuition of
Catholic theologies of grace: that divine grace works where and
how *it* wants, as *it* builds on, through, and with human nature.
The sins of humankind are neither cause of nor obstacle to God's
immense love, grace, and compassion, and neither are the religions
of humankind.[9]

Because there can be no grace known to humans that is not
experienced by humans as humans, then there can be no grace
known to humans that is not experienced by humans in and
through their cultures, genders, social locations, languages, and
religions.[10] No religion, as *Nostra Aetate* taught (n. 2), is without
grace, goodness, and truth, just as there is no human without grace,
because humanness itself is a gift of God's grace.[11] By reflecting on
the "gracious-ness" of religions, a Christian theology of religions
reflects on God's grace and its actions outside the realm of explicit
Christianity. Again, as *Nostra Aetate* taught (nn. 1 and 2), no religion is without imperfection, ignorance, and sin. Honesty and history demand that here we also include Christianity.

Christian theology must engage without imperialism and without naïveté in dialogue with non-Christians in order to name and
understand the workings of grace among them. Any theology of
religions is a Christian endeavor for Christianity's theological benefit, but it cannot exist without the cooperation of and dialogue
with non-Christians. They too unveil the mystery of God's gracious compassion for us, just as we hope we do for them.

The purpose of a Christian theology of religions, therefore, is
not primarily to assist in the church's missionary efforts but rather
to assist the whole church in understanding itself and its message,

because only then can Christians, sensitive to and better aware of grace's actions among others, respectfully, correctly, and sincerely proclaim God's gracious and definitive acts in Jesus of Nazareth.

What Would Be the Sources for a Latino/a Theology of Religions?

If we were to create a Latino/a theology of religions, we would need to look into the following three sources, each a complex web of diverse elements:

1. We need to consider Latino/a cultures, daily life, faith experiences, and perspectives, and the thematization of these in present-day U.S. Latino/a theologies. Because a Latino/a theology of religions has to be "Latino/a," then this is clearly nonnegotiable. With this consideration of culture, daily life, faith experiences, and perspectives must come an honest critique of Latino/a idols, limitations, and inabilities to respond to God's gracious compassion.[12]

2. We need to engage the non-Christian religions present among Latinos/as. Most of these religions are either native or African, and the religion with the most followers is called Lukumí.[13] It is known as Candomblé in Brazil, and is referred to as Santería in the United States and in Cuba, which is an unfortunate designation, because many—in and out of the religion—still insist on this misnomer, which was introduced by early twentieth-century whites who seemed incapable of understanding the Yoruba veneration of the *orishás* on its own terms.[14] It seems to me that a dialogue with Lukumí must move in two directions:

    a. Dialogue must be dialogue. In other words, the Lukumí religion must be welcomed as a partner and potential contributor to a better Christian understanding of God's grace and compassion, since this is the goal of any theology of religions. Consequently, the frequent Christian disdain for Lukumí and the equally frequent sense that this religion is doomed to fail and disappear must be erased among Christians; racist and colonial attitudes cannot be allowed to poison dialogue. Christians must honestly and sincerely strive to listen to and understand what God is compassionately doing in, for, and through this religion. And this implies getting to know and respect the religion from the perspective and the experience of the members.[15]

Just as Christians are very capable of attitudes that are unacceptable in their own religious tradition (e.g., cultural and ecclesial idolatry, racism, bigotry, and so forth), so are other religions capable of attitudes that are unacceptable in their own traditions. No religion has a monopoly on grace or a monopoly on sin. And if self-critique is a necessary element in the construction of a theology of religions, so is sincere mutual critique among religions—as long as it is mutual and as long as it is in a context of real, respectful dialogue. Otherwise we would not have moved much beyond the worst of the colonial days.

b. Christians must bring to the dialogue their own concerns and beliefs. For Christians, the revelation of God in and through Jesus the Christ is indeed revelation, the *definitive* revelation.[16] And although this belief in no way condones or promotes religious imperialism, it does mean that dialogue with non-Christians must result in the Christians' better understanding of what they sincerely claim to be the core of their faith tradition, and also result in making non-Christians better aware of what, why, and how Christians hold this belief. Agreement is not the necessary outcome of interreligious dialogue; mutual understanding and respect are. And what is just as important, interreligious dialogue is not the same as missionary discourse.

3. We need to recognize and dialogue with theologies of religions constructed, regardless of disciplinary label, throughout twenty centuries of Christian reflection by Latin American, Asian, African, European, and European American scholars:

- The reflections on non-Christians and their religions that began with Justin Martyr and Clement of Alexandria and spread throughout much of the patristic period are too important to be disregarded in any Catholic theology of religions today.
- The acknowledgment of the contributions from Christian history must pass through the theology of Ramón Llull and the rest of the theological production coming from the Iberian Middle Ages, where Christian dialogue and dealings with non-Christians were daily occurrences that led to still pertinent theological reflections.
- The works by Francisco de Vitoria, Bartolomé de Las Casas, Antonio de Montesinos, and Bernardino de Sahagún during the first century of Spanish imperial rule in the Americas are also important, as are the later colonial writings of Alfonso Sandoval, Epifanio Moiráns, and Francisco José de Jaca, and the contributions of those who wrote after independence.
- We must also go through Nicholas of Cusa in early modern Italy, as well as through the Jesuits Matteo Ricci and Roberto di Nobili; through our contemporaries Raimon Pannikar and Jacques Dupuis; and the recent works of other respected scholars, including F. X. Clooney, J. Hick, P. F. Knitter, D. Irarrázaval, A. Pieris, J. Martín Velasco, and L. Swidler.[17] I do not need to add that theologians require the contributions of historians and social and behavioral scientists, as well as the work of their own colleagues.
- We must carefully study Vatican II's conciliar documents, especially *Nostra Aetate* but also *Gaudium et Spes* and *Ad Gentes*, as well as statements by episcopal conferences in Africa, Asia, and Latin America.

- It is most important, of course, that we reflect on what the Hebrew Scriptures and the Christian New Testament teach us.

Together with this honorable and long line of theological scholarship on the meaning of non-Christian religions, we must weave in the historical contributions of theological reflection on grace and God, as well as Christian devotional material. And here I want to emphasize that, both in the U.S. Latino/a and in the Latin American contexts, as well as in other contexts throughout the church's long history, *how* Christians and non-Christians have understood and treated each other on a daily basis on street corners and street markets, in family homes, schools and city halls is a legitimate source for a theology of religions done *latinamente*.[18]

To construct, even if only the contours of, a Latino/a Catholic theology of religions requires, therefore, more than just looking at our own Latino/a cultural, religious, and theological backyard. It does not require our imitation, and much less our "translation," of someone else's methods, premises, and conclusions because this someone has only and inevitably written out of his/her own cultural, religious, and theological backyard. We can and must acknowledge and dialogue with others, but our work cannot be done *latinamente* by others, unless they choose to share in our perspectives and experiences.

Dialogue with the Lukumí Religion: Elements and Attitudes for a U.S. Latino/a Theology of Religions

Let us now place the preceding discussion on assumptions and sources for a U.S. Latino/a theology of religions in conversation with the Lukumí religion, and then let us see what results we get for a theology of religions constructed *latinamente*.

The Dialogue Partner: The Lukumí Religion in Synthesis

Lukumí is a religion brought to the Americas by Yoruba slaves, mostly during the nineteenth century. It is the same religion that, with minor variations, is known as Candomblé in Brazil.[19]

The reader must understand that, in the following very brief description of the Lukumí religion, I can offer only an extremely general, and consequently insufficient, presentation of the religion.

To the surprise of many (including many Latinos/as), the Lukumí religion claims that it is monotheistic.[20] Olòdúmaré, the supreme being, is arguably the only God in Lukumí belief. Known by several other designations (e.g., Olòrún [the "owner of the skies"] and Olòfín [the "owner of the power"]), the name Olòdúmaré expresses well a key Lukumí doctrine and insight into divinity (the name means "the one who bears the future in his hands"). This God is ultimately responsible for initiating the process of creation, although he is not the creator, and it is he who shapes the future according to his design and will. God is the supreme embodiment of all virtues, of all power, and of all wisdom; unfortunately, God is imaged exclusively as masculine.

This one God is not defined by compassion, mercy, or love, although Olòdúmaré is considered to possess all virtues, including compassion, mercy, and love. What ultimately defines God, besides the fullness of *ashé*, is power—the power to make the future, the power to create the *orishás,* the power to give life to the world, the power to obliterate the world, the power to do as he wishes. There are many sacred stories that teach that he is a God of power, not love.

God created the *orishás*[21] in order to rule the present and be responsible for it; it is to and through the *orishás* that we must address our concerns, and it is from the *orishás* that we expect assistance, reward, or punishment.

The *orishás* are not gods in the usual Western sense of the term; they are sacred beings, created by God (directly or indirectly), whose existence is now dependent on their receiving *ashé* from believers. The *orishás* are either masculine or feminine but not both, and they are subject to the same temptations and vices as humans, and to the same feelings, interests, virtues, and concerns. The *orishás* are limited in their knowledge and power, but they are immensely more powerful, knowledgeable, and wise than humans.

The most crucial element in Lukumí religion, and arguably the reason why the religion exists, is called in Yoruba *ashé*. The term *ashé* has no equivalent in any modern European language. An adequate approximation would say that *ashé* is the very principle of life, that which makes us *be* and *exist* as we are, socially and individually. *Ashé* is the stuff of divinity and the stuff of our humanity. *Ashé* is a spiritual principle, but it is also a material something that can be increased, acquired, decreased, etc.

The primary purpose of the religion is to keep *ashé* "flowing," in other words, to make sure that the *orishás* and human communities, and the individual persons who belong to them, keep receiving and giving *ashé* to one another.

God is God because God already has all the *ashé* he will ever need. This is why God is never worshipped in the Lukumí religion (beside the fact that he is in the future, and inaccessible to our worship). But the *orishás* and humans do require *ashé*, and thus most rituals have to do with "feeding" *ashé* to the *orishás*, or with our being "fed" *ashé* by them. The rituals of Lukumí might seem exotic, and perhaps occasionally repulsive, to many contemporary Christians. The liturgy is certainly elaborate, complex, and designed for the flowing of *ashé*. Rituals include offerings and prayers, as well as occasional animal sacrifices.

In the Lukumí religion there is a strong sense of moral right or wrong, but understood as that which contributes to or threatens the *ashé* of communities and individuals. There is no original sin and no action that, in itself, is necessarily good or evil. There is no need for redemption or salvation (these two notions are not part of the Lukumí religion). But the Lukumí do have a strong sense of communal responsibility and solidarity, even beyond death, developing much of their ethics from this emphasis and from their understanding of *ashé*.

There is such respect for life and for solidarity in the Lukumí religion that, when we die, we simply continue living in *Ikú*, the "place of the dead." There is no heaven and no hell, but continuation for as long as the dead are "fed" *ashé*.

The Lukumí religion has an extensive sacred literature, which must be spoken in order to be considered sacred (although many written, unofficial collections exist). Each sacred story is called a *pataki*, which is simply a didactic tale about something and whose purpose is to explain a doctrine, a ritual, or an ethical expectation. The truth of the *pataki* is in its core didactic message and in the behavior it elicits from the believer, and not in the story itself.

The believing community, called *ilé*, is always centered on a legitimate priest, has fully initiated members and a number of adepts who have not been fully initiated. The priest is crucial to the faith and ritual life of the community, but he/she is not allowed to impose his/her will on the community members. There can be no community without a priest, or a priest without a community. Both men and women can be priests, except, traditionally, in the priesthood of *Ifá*.

Having endured persecution, misguided and sometimes violent Catholic attempts at evangelization, and blatantly racist laws, Lukumí continues to grow. During the two centuries since its arrival from Nigeria, the religion has successfully streamlined itself while guaranteeing "orthodox," legitimate continuity with its Yoruba roots. Unfortunately, its forced conversation with Catholicism has often been a dialogue of the deaf, frequently leading nowhere and confirming the worst stereotypes on both sides.

In places such as Cuba, Brazil, and some U.S. areas with heavy Latino/a Caribbean populations, Lukumí is an omnipresent cultural perspective, even among those who might sincerely declare and believe themselves to be practicing Roman Catholics, Episcopalians, or Protestants.

As of today, the only attempts I know of Christian theologies of religion specifically grounded in the dialogue with Lukumí have been fewer than a dozen doctoral dissertations (including my own) and a handful of scholarly articles. Social scientists and historians, not Christian theologians, have been at the forefront of the study of Lukumí. The occasional references to this religion in theological works treating other issues does not make for a theology of religions.

The Starting Point of a Latino/a Theology of Religions in Dialogue with the Lukumí Religion

The starting point of a Latino/a theology of religions is daily reality, the reality experienced every day by the people. This affirmation, of course, requires other specifications and elaborations, but unfortunately I cannot delve into these right now.

Reality cannot be experienced except in daily life; this is what U.S. Latino/a theologians call *lo cotidiano*. It is only in daily life that we experience and live life. This is so self-evident that it seems strange when theologians look for great philosophical principles in order to ground the starting point of their theological constructs. *Lo cotidiano* is where we should go for our starting point.

In *lo cotidiano* of people, it should be honestly recognized, we find struggle and the fight for survival, racism, oppression, misunderstanding, colonial agendas, attempts at suppression, domestic violence, gender stereotypes, and other real but unethical and unacceptable behaviors. But in *lo cotidiano* we also find, with equal honesty, the goodness, the resilience, the courage, the dignity, the beauty, the wisdom, and the strengths of everyday people. *Lo cotidiano* is daily life as it is experienced and lived, but it is not just the raw data or the raw facts of daily life. *Lo cotidiano* is also the "knowing" and the "understanding" of daily reality jointly implied in and by the Spanish verbs *saber* and *conocer*.[22]

In *lo cotidiano* of many U.S. Latinos/as and Latin Americans we find a kind of popular inter-religious dialogue, whereby perspectives and elements of Christianity and of Lukumí are brought together in creative, tense, unexplained, and often mind-boggling syntheses, thereby becoming part of the shared cultural and social milieux of believers in both religions. The "roughness" of daily life shared by many Christians and Lukumís has often led them to this popular interreligious dialogue that somehow makes sense to them, even when their respective theologians might fault this dialogue as simplistic or unacceptable syncretism.

Christians and Lukumís, since the days of their first encounter in the late eighteenth century, have often treated each other in unfortunate and cruel ways, more specifically and frequently on the part of Christians, although many Lukumís in more recent times could also bear some of the blame. This is not the place to say whether Christians and Lukumís could have done differently. The experienced reality of the people who are Lukumí has little that is good to say about Christianity. And they have centuries of Christian mistreatment to point to. And yet, in spite of it all, Lukumís and Christians have engaged and continue to engage in this popular interreligious dialogue that has produced an inclusive religious universe often surprising and baffling to more theologically inclined Christians.

Can we have a Latino/a theology of religions that does not start with an acknowledgment of the terrors inflicted on Africans and natives in the name of Christianity, and that does not publicly name and repent from such horrible behavior? The daily reality of our people, in what it contributes to a theology of religions, must start with a recognition of wrongs inflicted and with real repentance.

Past offenses were fueled by racism and by an unacceptable sense of superiority—of white over black, of European over African, of Christian over Lukumí—and so a Catholic theology of religions today must make sure that in its constructs there is no implicit, and certainly no explicit, racist agenda or any sense of superiority over a non-Christian religion of African roots. Christian conviction in the definitive character of God's revelation in Christ does not require racist or imperial attitudes.

Sample Contributions of the Lukumí Religion
to a Latino/a Theology of Religions

If European, European American, and other white theologies of religions have been usually crafted on their encounter with Hinduism, Buddhism, Islam, and Judaism, then U.S. Latino/a and Latin American theologies of religions should first consider if their encounter with Lukumí, and with other African or native religions, should not be the grounds on which to build their theoretical constructs.

If dominant colonialism and triumphant imperial expansion were the non-innocent contexts and fuel for the white theologies of religions, in the case of Latino/a and Latin American theologies of religions it is slavery, marginalization, and oppressive colonization that provide the non-innocent context. In this latter context, the Lukumí religion stands out as the largest non-Christian religious universe that raises theological questions for Christians.

Let me briefly mention three sample contributions that the dialogue with Lukumí could make to a Latino/a theology of religions and to other very crucial areas in U.S. Latino/a theologies:

1. The Lukumí religion can and does offer the Latino/a Catholic theologian a challenging dialogue partner, one that can unexpectedly and uncomfortably challenge some naïvely held beliefs about both Latino/a identity and about non-Christian religions. For example:

    *   *U.S. Latino/a Lukumís are Latinos/as,* but they are neither Catholic nor Protestant. They are not devoted to the Virgin of Guadalupe, and today have little need of popular Catholicism, even of the Antillean brand. Latino/a Lukumís participate, because they are authentically Latinos/as, in the complex processes of Latino/a identity construction; but they point to identities that are neither white nor mestizo/a nor Christian.

    *   *Latino/a Lukumís are non-Christian Latinos/as.* As non-Christian Latinos/as, Lukumís again remind us that our

study of Latino/a identity needs to deal with *latinidad* in a manner that honestly acknowledges, and not just pays lip service to, the diversity and reality of non-Christian Latinos/as. Lukumí Latinos/as remind us of a long-standing interreligious dialogue that we have often subsumed or hidden under the categories of popular Catholicism, *mestizaje,* and even cultural identity, unfortunately forgetting the ugly side of racism, slavery, and Christian support of genocide. Lukumí Latinos/as won't let the Latino/a conscience "off the historical hook." We are asked to deal with our own idols and sins and not pretend that sinfulness is the exclusive monopoly of Spaniards or European Americans.

• The Lukumí, and other African and native religions among us, can help Latino/a theologians construct a theology of religions that is truly reflective of the diverse religious and cultural reality of Latinos/as—in other words, a theology of religions that acknowledges and elaborates on the Yoruba contributions to a Latino/a understanding of God, grace, compassion, humanness, etc., that can be shared by all Latino/a believers, and which could enlighten Christian reflection on those topics.

2. More concretely, our dialogue with the Lukumí religion should contribute to a Latino/a Catholic theology of religions that can affirm, with the Second Vatican Council, that there is "a spark of truth and wisdom" in the Lukumí and other non-Christian Latino/a religions. But in order to affirm honestly that as Christians we can find the spark of truth and wisdom in the Lukumí religion, we first need to delve into our own Christian understandings of truth and wisdom because maybe what we hold to be truth and wisdom are either needlessly restrictive or excessively relaxed, or perhaps culturally idolatrous. Our dialogue with the Lukumí religion, therefore, can help us reflect on what we Christians theologically mean by truth and wisdom.

3. The Lukumí religion could help Catholic theologians of religions wonder about the universal appeal or resonance of the Christian doctrines of original sin, redemption, salvation, and so on, which are so critical to the very core of the Christian religion. Can we claim universal validity for these doctrines, or can we even claim that these are universal human quests, when in our own backyard we have the Lukumí who have no such quests, no such doctrines, and yet are obviously *latinamente* human and religious?

4. We might expand some horizons of the Christian theology of grace if we would seriously dialogue with the Lukumí theology of *ashé*. And although it is very clear that *ashé* is not the equivalent of grace, there are many similarities and points of contact between the two doctrines.

   Although there is no direct translation of "*ashé*" into any modern European language, it might be approximated by the word "Life," with capital "L." *Ashé* is Life—the Life that is God, the Life that makes us be who and what we are, the Life that animates the entire cosmos. *Ashé* is the core of the Lukumí religion, and, to the degree that it can be accurately approximated as Life, it speaks to the Christian doctrine of grace. The Lukumí religion is an explicit and conscious effort at a creative dialogue between the human and the divine through participation and sharing in *ashé*. *Ashé* is always historical: Life from the past that becomes incarnate in the present in order to make possible the future. Can the theology of grace dialogue with, and perhaps learn from, the historicity and incarnational quality of *ashé*?

There are other possible contributions of the Lukumí religion to Christian theologies of religions, but the ones mentioned above will suffice for now.

And so, a U.S. Latino/a theology of religions can be constructed, and needs to be constructed, but it should be explicitly sensitive to the long history of reflection on non-Christian religions by Spanish and Latin American theologians. It must be respectful of U.S. Latino/a theological assumptions and sources, and it must be truly within the overall discipline known as "theology of religions."

Some among the third generation of U.S. Latino/a theologians will be interested in crafting a theology of religions *latinamente*. But I hope this theology will be done in sincere dialogue with Lukumí, Vodoun, Abakuá, Palo Mayombe, and the several other African religions in our midst, as well as in dialogue with the Latin American native religions that have now arrived in the United States and from the heritage of so many U.S. Latinos/as.

Notes

1. See *Annuario Pontificio 2004* (Vatican City: Lib. Editrice Vaticana, 2004).

2. See K. Davis and A. Hernández. "Hispanic Catholic Leadership: Key to the Future," in *Journal of Hispanic/Latino Theology* 10, no. 1 (2002): 37-60, for thorough and extensive statistics on the Latino/a presence in the U.S. Catholic Church and the clear consequences of this demographic growth.

3. The reader should be aware that by the term "Latino/a" I mean the U.S. population of Latin American ethnic, racial, or cultural roots (e.g., Mexican American, Puerto Rican, Cuban American, etc.). By "Latin American" I mean the populations of the twenty-one Latin American republics. I will not use the term "Hispanic." It is becoming increasingly less acceptable to the U.S. Latino/a population because it wrongly assumes that what the U.S. Latino/a communities have in common is only or mainly the heritage received from Spain. This colonial perspective disregards and minimizes the contributions of natives and Africans, who were and are as historically and culturally important as the Spaniards. The only way to make the term "Latino/a" gender inclusive is by the rather odd spelling.

4. There have been occasional references (in diocesan directives, and sometimes in local parishes) to African religions among U.S. Latinos/as. But most of these references, usually local and pastorally intended, have been

more diatribes against than efforts to understand, dialogue, or respect. Rarely have these ecclesial references reflected any awareness of or sympathy with Vatican II's *Nostra Aetate*. In official national magisterial documents there has been total silence. Among Catholic theologians there have been very few references to the African religions in our midst; most of these references have been typically tangential or secondary to the theological topics being discussed by the authors. For a more thorough explanation for this lack of sustained reflection on African religions by Cuban and Cuban American Catholic theologians, see my "Primeros pasos de una teología católica de las religiones afrocubanas," in *Filosofía, teología, literatura: Aportes cubanos en los últimos cincuenta años,* ed. R. Fornet-Betancourt (Aachen: Mainz Verlag, 1999), 212-30. It is a somewhat different story when, instead of African religions, we refer to native religions among U.S. Latinos/as. Here we find a growing interest among Catholic theologians, as well as a certain willingness (at parochial and diocesan levels) to adopt and adapt some elements of these religions in liturgical and catechetical contexts. Even here we wonder if the interest in native religions is focused on actual, living, present-day religions and on a sincere interest to dialogue with these present-day non-Christian religions, or if, instead, the focus is on Nahua (Aztec) and Maya religious and cultural elements as these might have in the *past* contributed to the formation of the largest segments of the U.S. Latino/a population's identity and culture, or to how these *past* contributions might enlighten this or that theological or pastoral issue today. I suspect the latter is the case, and if this is so then (again) the *living* native religions are relegated to contemporary theological irrelevance. In neither the dialogue with African religions nor the dialogue with native religions have U.S. Latino/a theologians developed a theology of living religions.

5. Estimates indicate that about one in every three Latin Americans, as well as one in every three U.S. Latino/a is racially (fully or partially) of African, although not exclusively Yoruba, descent. A higher proportion of Latin Americans and U.S. Latinos/as could be considered culturally (fully or partially) of African descent.

6. Although it is statistically evident that U.S. Latinos/as with Mexican and Central American native cultural or racial heritage form the majority of all U.S. Latinos/as, it is just as evident that the religions of their native ancestors have not significantly survived as *living* religions among most of them. Five centuries of Catholic influence and European dominance might help explain this fact. The Yoruba, however, have been in the Americas only for about two hundred years, and hence they were exposed to less Catholic influ-

ence. Their enslavement forced on them a set of cultural survival mechanisms that in time enabled their religion to live successfully past a century of slavery and racial and cultural discrimination. After slavery, without the legal and economic bounds imposed by that system, all sorts of Yoruba cultural, religious, and political societies were formed and some of these thrived. The survival of the Yoruba culture (e.g., language, music, family, etc.) greatly assisted the survival of the Yoruba religion, and vice versa. In the case of Cuba, the Yoruba were brought in very large numbers and soon, according to every census of the population taken during the nineteenth century, became half of the island's population. It is certain that today the Yoruba religion is the largest religion in Cuba and one of the largest in Brazil, with significant pockets in Puerto Rico, in some of the formerly British Caribbean islands, on the shores of Lake Maracaibo in Venezuela, and in the Chocó region of Colombia. It is also clear that the Yoruba religion, mostly as a result of immigration during the twentieth century, has successfully expanded into large U.S. and European urban areas where local non-immigrant populations have discovered and joined the religion as well as others from diverse (non-Cuban and non-Brazilian) immigrant groups. There are still significant portions of the Yoruba population in Nigeria who actively participate in their ancestral religion. In the absence of credible census figures on religious membership across the world, the best estimates place membership in the Yoruba religion worldwide at (at least) twenty million persons.

7. Theology of religions, as a discipline, has a vast scholarly bibliography to its credit. The following contemporary contributions have seemed richer to me because they suggest new lines of Christian thinking about non-Christian religions, clarify disciplinary foci, or make very important connections to other Christian theological disciplines: J. Dupuis, *Toward a Christian Theology of Religious Pluralism* (Maryknoll, N.Y.: Orbis Books, 1999); H. R. Schlette, *Die Religionen als Thema der Theologie* (Freiburg: Herder Verlag, 1963); J. M. Velasco, *El encuentro con Dios* (Madrid: Ed. Cristiandad, 1976); A. Race, *Christians and Religious Pluralism: Patterns in the Christian Theology of Religions* (Maryknoll, N.Y.: Orbis Books, 1982); D. G. Dawe and J. B. Carman, eds., *Christian Faith in a Religiously Plural World* (Maryknoll, N.Y.: Orbis Books, 1980); J. Hick and P. F. Knitter, eds., *The Myth of Christian Uniqueness: Towards a Pluralistic Theology of Religions* (Maryknoll, N.Y.: Orbis Books, 1987); P. F. Knitter, *No Other Name? A Critical Survey of Christian Attitudes Toward the World Religions* (Maryknoll, N.Y.: Orbis Books, 1985); J. Hick and B. Hebblethwaite, eds., *Christianity and Other Religions* (Philadelphia: Fortress Press, 1981); L. Swindler, ed., *Toward*

a Universal Theology of Religion (Maryknoll, N.Y.: Orbis Books, 1987); and numerous pertinent texts, not explicitly on a theology of religions but mostly on grace and soteriology, by K. Rahner, H. Küng, L. Boff, and E. Schillebeeckx.

8. Any Catholic theology of religions must, of course, be attentive to Vatican II's *Nostra Aetate*, while remaining familiar with other Vatican II documents (especially *Gaudium et Spes*, *Ad Gentes*, and *Dignitatis Humanae*). Paul VI's *Populorum Progressio* and *Evangelii Nuntiandi* offer important contributions, as does the Latin American bishops' *Puebla* document. The Asian and African conferences of bishops also have produced a number of texts that are very important for any Catholic theology of religions. All of these documents from the magisterium of the Church are explicit and unanimous in rejecting all forms of Christian imperialism, racism, or sense of superiority. The belief in the definitive revelatory character of Christianity, which these magisterial documents uphold and assume, is not grounds for justification of attitudes or theories that disrespect the members or the doctrinal contents and practices of non-Christian religions.

9. In this regard it is still very important and pertinent to keep in mind Paul Knitter's critical assessment of various Christian (Catholic and Protestant) attitudes toward non-Christian religions (see *No Other Name?* [n. 7]).

10. See O. Espín, "Grace and Humanness," in *We Are a People! Initiatives in Hispanic American Theology*, ed. R. S. Goizueta (Minneapolis: Fortress Press, 1992), 133-64.

11. Was this not one of Karl Rahner's great contributions to the theology of grace? Besides examining the expected Rahnerian texts from his *Theological Investigations* and other explicitly theological works, the reader might do well to carefully reflect on Rahner's "spiritual" writings. wherein he often applies and develops practically much of his own theology of grace; for example: *The Love of Jesus and the Love of Neighbor* (New York: Crossroad, 1983); and *Encounters with Silence* (Westminster, Md.: Newman Press, 1966). For a good synthetic presentation of Rahner's theology of grace and its many connections with U.S. Latino/a theologies of grace, which in turn "feed" and make possible a Latino/a theology of religions, see M. H. Díaz, *On Being Human: U.S. Hispanic and Rahnerian Perspectives* (Maryknoll, N.Y.: Orbis Books, 2001).

12. There is a large and easily accessible bibliography from the social and behavioral sciences, as well as from history, on numerous aspects of U.S. Latino/a culture and religion. Books, journals, and articles on and from Latino/a *theological* scholarship are also easily accessible. This is not the place

to include long introductory bibliographies on topics with which most readers are already familiar.

13. The available bibliography on Lukumí/Candomblé (mostly in Spanish, Portuguese, and English) is large. The Yoruba-language bibliography, difficult to access outside of Nigeria, is also ample and important. Among the better introductory texts to the religion are M. Cros Sandoval, *La religión afrocubana* (Madrid: Ed. Playor, 1975); J. M. Murphy, *Santería: An African Religion in America* (Boston: Beacon Press, 1988); M. A. Mason, *Living Santería: Rituals and Experiences in an Afro-Cuban Religion* (Washington: Smithsonian Institution Press, 2002); J. García Cortez, *El Santo/La Ocha: Secretos de la religión Lucumí* (Miami: Ed. Universal, 1971); L. Cabrera, *El Monte* (Miami: Ed. Universal/Chicherekú, 1970); V. J. Berkenbrock, *A experiência dos orixás: Um estudo sobre a experiência religiosa no Candomblé* (Petrópolis [Brazil]: Ed. Vozes, 1997); W. Bascom, *Sixteen Cowries: Yoruba Divination from Africa to the New World* (Bloomington: Indiana University Press, 1980); Y. M. Alves Velho, *Guerra de orixá. Um estudo de ritual e conflito* (Rio de Janeiro: Zahar Editores, 1975); R. Lachatañeré, *El sistema religioso de los afrocubanos* (Havana: Ed. de Ciencias Sociales, 1992); R. E. Harding, *A Refuge in Thunder: Candomblé and Alternative Spaces of Blackness* (Bloomington: Indiana University Press, 2000); F. Ortiz, *Ensayos etnográficos* (Havana: Ed. de Ciencias Sociales, 1984); idem, *Los negros brujos* (Miami: Ed. Universal, 1973); G. E. Brandon, *The Dead Sell Memories: An Anthropological Study of Santería in New York City* (Ann Arbor, Mich.: University Microfilms International, 1989); J. García Cortez, *Pataki: Leyendas y misterios de los orishas africanos* (Miami: Ed. Universal, 1980); J. M. Murphy and M.-M. Sanford, eds. *Òsun across the Waters: A Yoruba Goddess in Africa and the Americas* (Bloomington: Indiana University Press, 2001); Ó. Lele, *The Secrets of Afro-Cuban Divination* (Rochester, Vt.: Destiny Books, 2000); idem, *Obí: Oracle of Cuban Santería* (Rochester, Vt.: Destiny Books, 2001); idem, *The Diloggún: The Orishas, Proverbs, Sacrifices and Prohibitions of Cuban Santería* (Rochester, Vt.: Destiny Books, 2003); B. I. Karade, *The Handbook of Yoruba Religious Concepts* (York Beach, Me.: Weiser Books, 1994); O. Ecún, *Addimú: Ofrenda a los orichas* (Miami: Ed. SIBI, 1988); idem, *Oricha. Metodología de la religión yoruba* (Miami: Ed. SIBI, 1985); O. G. Cacciatore, *Dicionário de cultos afro-brasileiros* (Rio de Janeiro: Ed. Forense Universitária, 1977); J. E. dos Santos, *Os nagô e a morte* (Petrópolis [Brazil]: Ed. Vozes, 1977); F. A. M. Adéwálé-Somadhi, *Fundamentals of the Yorùbá Religion* (San Bernardino, Ca.: Ilé Òrúnmìlà Communications, 1993).

14. The Spanish term *santería* means the exaggerated or superstitious veneration of saints (Real Academia Española, *Diccionario de la lengua española* [Madrid: Real Academia Española, 1992, 21st ed.]). During the colonial period in Cuba, police would break into and wreak havoc on *ilés* of the Lukumí, because the practice of the religion was legally banned and severely punished. As a defensive tactic, many Lukumí began to use images of Catholic saints that they thought were somehow related (often by superficial or tangential links) to the *orishás*. Thus, if the police raided an *ilé*, all they would find would be Catholic images and symbols. Although these appeared exaggerated, even by colonial standards, they nevertheless fit in with white racist assumptions of the slaves' ignorance and inclination to superstition. ("Catholic" superstition was *not* beyond what the authorities could legally tolerate in an officially Catholic colony.) This Lukumí practice became acceptable among later generations of believers, especially during periods of legal persecution and social repression. The term *santería* came to be used for the religion, especially by early twentieth-century white Cuban scholars who thought this creative (and successful) defense mechanism defined the Lukumí religion. Indeed, elaborate theories of syncretism were created (and are still repeated today) to explain Lukumí as ultimately a Cuban mixture of the Yoruba religion with Catholicism. Unfortunately and needlessly, the use of "Santería" and many of the syncretic explanations have become commonplace among white U.S. academics. Today, most members of the religion refer to it by the term Lukumí or, less frequently, by the late colonial expression *Regla de Osha*. The use of "Santería" among its members tends to be more for the benefit of outsiders. In the United States, many Lukumí have a growing sense that the term "Santería" ultimately denigrates their religion and perpetuates a misunderstanding that was historically justifiable, but no longer necessary. We should also recall that given the Cuban and Cuban American cultural propensity to play down all religious affiliations and their demands, there is a large segment of these populations, not formally affiliated with Lukumí but in occasional attendance at *ilés*, who commonly refer to Lukumí as "Santería." I received this information and explanation personally from the late Prof. Lydia Cabrera, who was one of the world's foremost authorities on the religion; several Lukumí priests later confirmed Cabrera's points for me.

15. Respect and dialogue are attitudes explicitly taught and required by *Nostra Aetate*. For both dialogical and dismissive attitudes toward Lukumí among Cuban and Cuban American theologians, see my "Primeros pasos de una teología católica de las religiones afrocubanas" (n. 5, above).

16. Some authors (e.g., J. Hick and others) have suggested that, given

our religiously plural world, Christian theologies need to rethink their claims concerning the uniqueness of Jesus and Christian revelation. See, as an example of their position, J. Hick and P. F. Knitter, eds., *The Myth of Christian Uniqueness* (n. 7, above). It seems undeniable, however, that the majority of Christians in the world would have serious difficulty with anything short of the statement I just made. That God may have spoken to/with others is not the question; rather, the definitive character of Christian revelation is. In any case, this is not the place to engage in this conversation, but it most certainly is the place for acknowledging that, regardless of whether we think they are theologically correct or incorrect, for most Christians interreligious dialogue cannot compromise what they hold to be central to their religion. In other words, interreligious dialogue cannot ignore the real faith of real people except at the risk of becoming a conversation among specialists who represent no one but themselves.

17. This list is not limited to these scholars. There are many distinguished authors (in Europe, Africa, Asia, and Latin America) whose works can and should be regarded with attention.

18. U.S. Latino/a theologians have been (and still are) at the forefront of international theological reflection on popular religion as a legitimate and necessary theological source. As examples, see R. Fornet-Betancourt, ed., *Kapitalische Globalisierung und Befreiung: Religiöse Erfahrungen und Option für das Leben* (Aachen: Verlag für Interkulturelle Kommunikation, 2000); idem, ed., *Glaube an der Grenze: Die US-amerikanische Latino-Theologie* (Freiburg im Breisgau: Verlag Herder, 2002); O. Espín, *The Faith of the People: Theological Reflections on Popular Catholicism* (Maryknoll, N.Y.: Orbis Books, 1997); O. Espín and M. H. Díaz, eds., *From the Heart of Our People: Latino/a Explorations in Catholic Systematic Theology* (Maryknoll, N.Y.: Orbis Books, 1999).

19. See the bibliography on Lukumí in note 13, above.

20. This monotheistic claim, of course, is the source of much debate, division, and controversy among those who study the Lukumí religion, as well as among its members. Is Lukumí truly monotheistic in the sense that it believes in the existence of only one God? Are not the *orishás* commonly worshipped and regarded as gods and goddesses? But are the *orishás* not dependent on human offerings of *ashé* in order to survive, thereby demonstrating that they do not possess the fullness of *ashé* and, hence, that they are finite? The key issue, in my view, is the assumed definition of divinity (i.e., what do we mean when we say "god"?). Is a traditional Yoruba definition to be used, or is a Western (originally white and arguably Christian) definition

of divinity preferred? Do we appeal to definitions, regardless of source, or do we attempt, instead, to appeal to a more performative approach? These questions and issues need to be considered before concluding that Lukumí is monotheistic. In my own work I have concluded that the monotheistic claim is valid, but only if a traditional Yoruba definition of divinity is contrasted with a typically Western definition of "god." See my *Evangelización y religiones negras,* vols. I-IV (Rio de Janeiro: Ed. PUC/RJ, 1984); and also E. B. Idowu, *God in Yoruba Belief* (London: Blackwell, 1962); and J. S. Mbiti, *Concepts of God in Africa* (London: S.P.C.K., 1970).

21. The term *orishá* is here written as it "sounds" in Yoruba. All other Yoruba terms in this article are also rendered in phonetic transliteration. Contemporary Yoruba is written in the Roman alphabet, but it uses a wealth of other diacritic symbols and accents not easily understood (and not employed) by people who speak English, Spanish, or Portuguese.

22. *Saber* and *conocer* can both be translated into English as "to know." In Spanish, however, they are often distinct in suggesting the "factual knowing" (*saber*) and the "understanding" (*conocer*) implied and involved in every act of knowing. The connection between *lo cotidiano* and these two Spanish ways of referring to knowing were brought to my attention by Prof. Nancy Pineda-Madrid.

4

We Are What We Are

Africanness and Slavery as Sources for Latino/a Theology

The time has come for Latino/a theology and for theologians to "re-cognize" the evident presence and enduring heritage of Africa in U.S. Latino/a cultures and blood. We are not just descendants of natives, or *mestizos/as*, or Iberian-descendant *criollos/as*. We are also, and as much, descendants of Africans, blacks and *mulatos/as*.[1] At least one-third of all U.S. Latinos/as are descendants of Africans, and this proportion is rising in the Latin American lands of our ancestors.

To forget the contributions and presence of Africa in our cultures and in our blood would amount to a self-mutilation that could result, as it has begun to result, in a mutilated and unsustainable Latino/a identity. To forget Africa leads to a theology that can hide and suppress a substantial part of our communities' rich and complex roots. Paraphrasing what a popular song once said, "We are what we are, and what we are needs no excuses." Africa and its heritage are part of who we are, and there is no denying or playing it down any longer.

Now, I am not the first one to suggest this. Many distinguished Latino/a scholars in the United States have been reminding us, for

This paper was presented in the section on Latino/a Theologies at the 2006 convention of the Catholic Theological Society of America, in San Antonio, Texas.

a very long time, of our complex racial and cultural reality, and, more specifically, of our Africanness. Theologians, however, have not been among these scholars until rather recently. Nevertheless, it has now become evident that we can no longer proceed in the construction of U.S. Latino/a theology as if Africa and Africanness were irrelevant to us.

Latino/a Cultural Reality:
African Slaves and White *Criollos/as*

Let me explain why I suggest "Africanness" instead of "blackness" as the more adequate description of this source of our *latinidad*.[2]

Latinos/as and the Latin Americans at the origins of our communities are the result of centuries of cultural and racial mixings—some of these willing and some of these violent. We cannot simply speak of being black, in the American sense of the term, because many of us who in fact are the heirs of Africa have a broad range of skin colors that do not challenge, deny, or hide the Africanness of our cultural identities but which, to the outsider, might not appear to witness to our African heritage. Of course, there are black Latinos/as, just as there are *mulatos/as* in all shades of the chromatic range, and even apparently white Latinos/as who will feel personally addressed by the politely devious question, *¿y tu abuelita dónde está?*[3]

Mixture of blood and ancestries seems historically to be the rule and process that gave birth to all Latino/a communities, and this process has included the blood of Africa. This, in turn and very importantly, implies that if we speak of some Latino/a cultures being *mestizas/os* (and of members of these cultures, even when racially white, as being very much *mestizos/as* by culture), then we must also speak of other Latino/a cultures as being *mulatas/os* (and of members of these cultures as being very much *mulatos/as* by culture). Because the processes of racial and cultural mixing continue to this day among U.S. Latinos/as and among Latin Americans, we may reasonably bet that the future will not bring the demise of either *mestizaje* or *mulataje*, but an increase that will necessarily require our recognition of a growing social and cultural U.S. Latino/a reality: persons and communities who are the result of the mixing of *mestizos/as* and *mulatos/as*. This mixture had already appeared in colonial Latin America, and has remained commonplace in our ancestral continent, but it has become increasingly more common in the United States.

I am in no way denying or minimizing race and racial issues, because these certainly exist among us; I am pointing out, however, that how Africa, Africanness, race, etc. historically and culturally appear among U.S. Latinos/as and Latin Americans is not coextensive with or equal to the same issues within the traditional U.S. racial divide between black and white. For better or worse, in our specific contexts, these issues are even more complex and at times result in ideological attempts at denial or cooptation. Africa, Africanness, race, and so forth are very much a part of U.S. Latino/a reality, but they are reflective of who we are as part, even crucially important parts, of a mixture—racial or cultural. And it is important to keep this historical fact in mind.

And, yes, we do have our "Oreos" too, as well as ideological manipulations of race that have resulted in all sorts of historical atrocities and cultural mutilations. I again insist that these should not be minimized or ignored; on the contrary, we must take Africa's blood and cultures, and the slavery of Africans, very seriously as a source of U.S. Latino/a theology. But we must go about it in ways that authentically reflect our own histories and contexts and not someone else's.

Most of us—Latinos/as and Latin Americans, heirs of Africa—bring Africa in our souls if not always in our skins, although very many of us also proudly display Africanness in both soul and skin. Puerto Ricans, Cubans, Dominicans, Venezuelans, Colombians, Panamanians, Brazilians, many Central Americans, and even Mexicans can and do know that Africanness is as much part of them as the Iberian heritage of those who dominated our colonial communities and who succeeded in implanting their dominant language, religion, and culture.[4]

Skin color alone does not limit, indicate, or preserve the presence of Africa among Latinos/as. *Africanness* does: the culture, the memory, the history, the heritage—all in and through that extraordinarily messy, sometimes violent, and always complex historical mixing of peoples and cultures that we are. Africanness is present in our *lo cotidiano*: in our self-understanding, in foods and vocabulary, in dress styles and family formations, in social behaviors and artistic expressions. Africanness is everywhere among us, molding us and imprinting in our cultural souls the maternal embrace of Africa, even when our skin color might betray the presence of other ancestries in the historical mixing processes from which we resulted.

The African presence in us did not arrive by way of tourism or voluntary immigration. The Africanness of our identity came with slavery, the system and the millions of humans, mostly Yoruba, who were violently captured and transported to Latin America. There they were forced to work, reproduce, and die for the benefit of the Iberian and *criollo/a* white dominant minorities, who did their best to "morally" justify the atrocities of slavery, which they inflicted on millions of defenseless human beings in the name of Christianity and the Christian God.[5]

Consequently, to acknowledge our Africanness might not require black skin, but it most certainly *demands* the acceptance of our roots in the horrors and violence of slavery, in the blood and sufferings of slaves, and in the terrible cultural, and sometimes legalized, racism that continued after the end of the slave-holding period. The acknowledgment that our roots include slavery and slaves must be transparent and consequent—"we are what we are, and what we are needs no excuses." We too are the children of Africa—but of enslaved, violated, and tortured Africa in Latin America. This Africa, with pride, wisdom, and savvy, as well as with extraordinary efforts, managed to preserve its cultures and sometimes its languages, religions, and identities, and has generously contributed these to Latin America and to many U.S. Latino/a communities. Africa and Africans, and the experience of slavery and racism, have developed into that very complex historical and cultural mixture of which we are the present result.

On the other side of this coin, we too are heirs to the racist "whitening" policies of so many Latin American countries. These policies were explicitly instituted during the second half of the nineteenth century and the first half of the twentieth with the publicly and officially stated intention of reducing the percentage of African descendants among us and of "cleaning up" the Latin American—and by extension U.S. Latino/a—bloodlines of all "vestiges of the savage."[6]

We are heirs of the slaves and of the Africanness they brought to our side of the world, but we are also heirs to the culture of racial bigotry brought by the Iberians and perpetuated by the white *criollos/as*. Whether we are embarrassed by this dual heritage or not, it is there and it is ours. The cultural reality of many U.S. Latinos/as is as much heir to this dual history as to the cultural realities of our Latin American forebears and contemporaries. "We are what we are," and we had better admit it.

Africanness and Slavery as Sources for Latino/a Theology

If we acknowledge Africa, Africanness, and slavery as part of our Latino/a heritage and identity, then these must become sources for Latino/a theologizing. And I insist on this because U.S. Latino/a theology has distinguished itself for its thematic and methodological emphases on identity and culture, on sociohistorical reality and the struggle for justice, and on the people's religion. We have frequently insisted on the role of these as sources of theology. Consequently, we would adulterate our theology if we were to continue ignoring or minimizing in our theological constructions the heritage and the consequent issues that have been raised here.

We have, over the past three decades, written eloquently on

Amerindians and *mestizos/as*. We had to, because much of what we are is their heritage in us. We have also written on the Iberian heritage; we had to and for the same reason. So it is now time that we break out of another racist, ideological prison and responsibly assume Africa, Africanness, and slavery, and again for exactly the same reason: because we are these too.

As one way of suggesting methodologically how our Africanness and slavery can become sources for our theologizing, let me focus on one specific contribution of Africa that is so evident among many U.S. Latino/a communities: religion, and, more specifically, the African religions among us. Although I am here referring to religion as a vehicle of Africanness and of African contributions, I am in no way suggesting that a thorough study of these can be adequately successful without careful study of other cultural, historical, sociological, and anthropological data. No matter how important religion is culturally, it does not exhaust all that is conveyed in and through culture.

There are two sides to this fontal approach to Africanness and slavery by way of religion.

Challenging a Repeated Understanding of Latino/a Identity

I need not present here again the arguments for understanding a people's religion ("popular religion") as a privileged, although not exclusive, bearer of identity and culture in a community's history. I have written extensively on this subject. Here I only need to restate that any popular religion plays a complex historical, cultural role—a role that shapes and marks a people's cultural identity beyond and beneath the institutional, social role the same religion might have in society. The same is true for the African religions brought by the slaves to the Americas.

The list of these religions must include, first and foremost, Lukumí and Candomblé (slightly different from each other peripherally but substantially the same Yoruba religion in the Americas); and then we must necessarily include Vodoun (originally from

Benin, but as it developed in Haiti, the Dominican Republic, and northern Brazil); and a number of numerically smaller religions such as Abakuá, Palo Mayombe, the Shangó tradition (of Trinidad), the Ayé tradition (of the Lake Maracaibo region of Venezuela), and so on. The list would grow considerably if we added the religions born in the Americas but with some African parentage (e.g., Dominican Olivorism, Brazilian Umbanda, Jamaican Obeah, and others). For most scholars and nonscholars in the United States, it comes as a surprise that most of these religions are already present here and that Lukumí-Candomblé is now the largest non-Christian religion in the United States, having broken beyond its historical boundaries within the Cuban-American and Brazilian-American communities.

When we decide to acknowledge Africanness and slavery as sources of Latino/a theology, and especially when we choose to look at African religions in the Americas as privileged bearers of African culture and identity and as witnesses to the slaves' history of suffering and struggle and their contributions, we must confront and critique the notion—so often repeated among Latino/a theologians—that U.S. Latino/a identity is religiously rooted exclusively in Christianity. Therefore, not only the notion of all of us being *mestizos/as* needs deep and serious revamping but also the idea that all of us are somehow culturally or religiously Christian. To think, therefore, that our *latinidad* is exclusively grounded on *mestizaje* and on Christianity is not only incorrect historically and culturally, but it is also an ideologically manipulative instrument intent on hiding Africa, Africanness, and slavery from the present of those whose history cannot be understood otherwise. To put it bluntly, to continue to repeat as self-evident or as unquestionable that U.S. Latino/a identity is only or mainly *mestiza/o* and Christian is to play the game of the dominant Eurocentric ideology because we would be hiding ourselves from ourselves while mutilating part of who we are and thereby contributing to our own alienation.

The existence and continued vitality of Lukumí-Candomblé, of

Vodoun, and of other African popular religions among us is a very explicit sign that much of what U.S. Latino/a theology has written on identity and culture either needs some profound rethinking, or it needs to be rejected as ideologically compromised.

The hundreds of thousands of U.S. Latinos/as who practice any one of these popular religions are still Latinos/as, yet not Christian, at least not in the Christian sense of this term, and they cannot be ignored in a theology that insistently claims to be Latina/o because it speaks from the Latina/o reality and experience. Latina/o reality and experience are not all *mestiza/o*, all *criolla/o*, or all Christian, or any combination thereof.

In specific local Latino/a communities it is perfectly adequate to continue to speak of Christianity and *mestizaje* as pillars of their identity and culture; but specific local communities are specific local communities. It is only when we look at and methodologically incorporate the local communities from all across the country that we can speak of a shared or common national Latino/a identity. As I suggested in 2004 at a CTSA convention,[7] we need a Latino/a theology of religions that would dialogically engage the non-Christian *within* us and not just "among" us, or we risk turning all our talk of contextualization, identity and culture, and of social reality, into an ideological artifact worthy of the trash bin.

To acknowledge and methodologically incorporate Africanness and slavery as sources of our theologizing requires, therefore, that we first broaden our Latino/a notions of identity and culture in order to acknowledge, receive, and map Latino/a reality—a crucially indispensable source of our theologizing—in its real complexity. We need to do justice to the non-Christian among us, as well as to those whose ancestry lies in Africa and not in Europe or in the peoples of the preconquest Americas. The non-Christian religions with African roots remind us of our truer identity as Latinos/as and convey to us the spiritual and cultural values of the slaves and their descendants—a conveyance that, historically, made us into what and who we are. A study of Latino/a cultures would unveil how deeply these spiritual and cultural values have impacted who and what we are, how much they have mixed with the *criollo/a* and the *mestizo/a*, and how widely present Africanness has been among U.S. Latinos/as.

I hasten to add, however, that it would be a huge methodological error to assume that Africanness and slavery, conveyed to us mainly, but not exclusively, through the popular religions with African roots, can be simplistically identified or made coextensive with the non-Christian. That would also violate historical data as well as cultural and social realities. Furthermore, the simplistic identification of the African with the non-Christian could be construed or manipulated to mean, at least among some Christians, that Africanness and the experience of the slaves are "inferior" or tangential, and thus easily dismissed as other, pagan, or strange, clearly only peripherally ours and, at worst, something to be superseded because they are no more than the vestige of an unfortunate past. So there is more to this than the challenge our Africanness poses to the oft-repeated notion of Latino/a identity as *mestiza/o* and Christian.

Contributing to a More Comprehensive Latino/a Identity

The popular religions with African roots teach us more because they have done more, culturally and historically. Any religion is more and conveys more than its specifically spiritual, creedal, liturgical, or revelatory contents. Indeed, it can be easily demonstrated that none of these contents is ever conveyed, received, or understood except within cultural frameworks that were themselves molded in and by history and other social and political forces. No religion is ever only its sincerely held beliefs, rituals, spiritual experiences, ethical codes, etc. Any religion includes these, of course, and its social success will greatly depend on the power of these to convince. But all religions are also a set of intersecting culturally and historically shaped matrices that in turn transmit and shape the cultures in which the religions find themselves.

In this specific role as shaper of culture, the African religions have contributed greatly to Latin America and to U.S. Latinos/as. This is true, culturally and historically speaking, of the Dominican Republic, Haiti, Brazil, Puerto Rico, Cuba, and of significant regions of Venezuela, Colombia, and Panama; of smaller but still important areas of Peru, Ecuador, Costa Rica, Nicaragua, and Honduras; and of Jamaica and other island nations of the English-, French-, and Dutch-speaking Caribbean. More to our point, this is clearly and consequently true and applicable to U.S. Latino/a populations whose cultural ancestry lies in these Latin American countries. Could a U.S. Puerto Rican, a Dominican American, or a Cuban American—to name but three of the larger U.S. Latino/a communities—understand her/himself without Africanness and the cultural contributions of African religions any more than their Latin American forebears? Worldviews, customs, food items and preparation, music, family styles, gender roles, etc., none particularly "religious," have been influenced by Africanness as conveyed culturally by African religions. For example, anyone who has ever participated in a Lukumí *tambor* knows that much of what in time became popular music[8] can trace its origins back to many of the sacred rhythms in honor of the *orishás*.

Assumptions about matters specifically spiritual or ethical, for example, African religious inclusiveness, cross the commonly regarded boundaries of Christian or African religions, and permeate the cultural worldviews of very many Latinos/as.[9] African religious inclusiveness, although rarely named as such, is a cultural commonplace among most U.S. Latinos/as of Cuban, Puerto Rican, and Dominican ancestry. Actively participating in more than one religious tradition at the same time, even while claiming membership in one or another, while also demonstrating uncanny success at managing the "theological dissonances" that multiple participation would imply for a Christian (or European) context, is one indication of the African religious inclusiveness of the (Caribbean) Latino/a cultural worldview. Cuban religion scholars have referred to this mindset as "religious *ajiaco*," a reference to the popular Cuban stew that includes a great variety of disparate ingredients.

Many more examples could be mentioned of the contributions made by African religions to our cultural Africanness, which was brought to the Americas by the slaves. African inclusiveness, and so many other gifts from Africa, I must insist, were not brought "to us" as if a Latino/a "we" existed prior to the arrival of the slaves and their descendants. No. The Latino/a "we" is precisely the result of the long process of mixing that gave birth to "us." In other words, what we received from Africa did not become grafted onto an already-existing Latino/a trunk but became one of its roots. We are the heirs and result of the mixing of Africanness as much as of the Iberian, and this brings us back to the question of Latino/a identity.

We already saw that whatever we understand as Latino/a identity cannot be limited to the native, the *mestizo/a*, the *criollo/a,* or the Christian. Our roots are not just native, Iberian, or Christian, or a combination of these. Historically by way of slavery, we Latinos/as are also African, descendants of Africans, and non-Christian—mainly traditional Yoruba and Fon. The process of mixing all of these native, African, Iberian, Christian, and Yoruba or Fon cultural, religious, historical, and racial elements in time gave rise to what we are. "We are what we are, and what we are needs no excuses."; but it does need acknowledgment and acceptance. Our Africanness should make it possible for us to acknowledge and accept more comprehensively, with an attitude of inclusiveness, our shared and mixed identity, but without despising or repressing any side of it as better or more acceptable to the dominant.

We must not commit against ourselves the racism that others have often engaged in when defining us, even when the attempt to define us has come from friendly quarters with good and even supportive intentions. "We are what we are," and it is we who must define who, what, and why we are.

Identity is not a given of nature but a historical, cultural construct of human communities. We define ourselves, first and foremost, for ourselves, to understand ourselves; and then, secondarily, to distinguish ourselves from others and to help them understand us.

In the case of Latinos/as, we are still using identity constructs inherited from our Latin American forebears, as perhaps we had to. While infrequent contacts occurred among U.S. Latino/a communities, the use of Latin American identity constructs might have been justified and perhaps inevitable. The "other" for all of us, for nearly two centuries, was the European American whom we understood as white, racist, Protestant, dominant, strange, and unfriendly. But increasingly during the second half of the twentieth century we began to notice that among us too there were whites, racists, Protestants, and other Latino/a groups that, for our particular community, seemed strange and potentially unfriendly. As the decades progress, Latinos/as have nationally become increasingly aware of the enormous diversity we represent, and yet we are also becoming painfully aware that we have neither the categories nor the leadership to aid in our shared construction of a national Latino/a identity that is truly inclusive of the diversity we are. Unless we fall into the trap of dominance among ourselves, one group imposing its categories and identity on the rest, we are left with two alternatives: either we stop regarding ourselves as a community of communities (as we have for half a century, trying to build alliances and common approaches to a myriad of issues that affect us all), or we get to work creating the categories and leadership that, respecting our diversity as a community of communities, will allow us all to construct and own a shared national Latino/a identity that avoids Latin American categories and is expressive of what we are.

A theoretical opening in what we could call the "theology of identity," came in the 1970s with Virgilio Elizondo's work on *mestizaje* and on Jesus as a *mestizo*. Many of us jumped at the possibility of constructing a shared national identity through *mestizaje*, but *mestizaje* has proven itself incapable of the inclusiveness that our shared identity demands. *Mestizaje* hides and silences as much as it unveils, and it ignores completely that at least one-third of all Latinos/as have no native blood (racially or culturally), thereby rendering *mestizaje* useless as a truly national identity category. But the same is the case were we to opt for the parallel category of *mulataje*. Attempts were made to use such categories as "borderlands," "*nepantlah,*" etc.—but none proved any better than *mestizaje*. Others have tried to create a theology of Latino/a identity by compiling a list of its elements, in the hope that time would mold them into a coherent analytical category. It is the more common approach today to list identity markers to indicate our complex reality, but the description of the parts of a mosaic is not and can never be equal to the whole. Will this listing of identity markers prove fruitful? Perhaps.

We are, therefore, at a crucial moment in U.S. Latino/a theology, because identity has been an enormously important source of our theologizing and because the categories we have used for decades to reflect on and theologize on our identity have proven to be insufficient at best or just plain useless for a national theology. The fact that we need to highlight African elements (cultural, religious, historical, etc.) is an indication of how our old reflection on Latino/a identity as *mestizaje* has proven to be incomplete, sometimes ideologically manipulative, and simply no longer sufficient or acceptable for our community of communities.

Latinos/as of many communities now live in all fifty states. They work together, fight for the same rights, often share the same neighborhoods, listen to the same national Latina/o media, and so on, and can no longer pretend that any one of our communities can define what/who we are *nationally* and, increasingly, not even what/who we are regionally. Families, so important for all Latinos/as, are now being established in increasing numbers by Latinos/as from different communities. What will their children, and their children's children be if this trend continues? New York is no longer, *latinamente* speaking, a Puerto Rican city; nor is Miami a Cuban city; and Los Angeles will one day soon be much more than a Mexican metropolis. The future is arriving with even more diversity, sometimes also speaking Portuguese, and forcing us to define ourselves as we are and not as we wished we were.

Africa, Africanness, and the experience and history of slaves are all part of what we are. And we *must*, if we want to see the consolidation of a national Latino/a identity, acknowledge and accept that this identity must consciously embrace the contributions of our present and historical Africanness.

Notes

1. In English and among many African Americans, the term "mulatto" carries offensive connotations. In Spanish and Portuguese, however, and among U.S. Latinos/as and Latin Americans, the term *mulato/a* (so spelled) not only does *not* carry an offensive connotation but has in fact now become a sign of pride and identity. I am using this term here according to its use among Latinos/as and Latin Americans.

2. *Latinidad* literally means "Latino/a-ness." This, evidently, brings up the question of identity. For an extended treatment of identity and the construction of identity (far from any essentialist approach), see my "*Humanitas*, Identity, and Another Theological Anthropology," which appears as chapter 2 of the present volume. See also the bibliography cited there.

3. Literally, "Where is your grandmother?" The question refers to one's racial ancestry, and assumes that there is more to it than present-day appearance. The question reminds me of the statement by Cuban scholar H. Portell Vilá, who remarked that in Cuba, *el que no tiene de congo tiene de carabalí* (lit., "whoever doesn't have Congolese blood has Calabarese," implying that in Cuba the blood of Africa is present in and mixed with all—even those who today appear racially white). Portell Vilá was exaggerating somewhat, but he did make his point regarding long-standing and widespread racial mixing in Cuba, despite all attempts to make present appearances deny the facts of racial history.

4. I am amazed at how little most Mexicans and Mexican Americans know of the African presence in Mexican history, of African contributions to Mexican culture, and of the ongoing presence and contributions of African descendants in today's Mexico. Indeed, it seems that in Mexico it is broadly assumed that if one claims Africanness as one's heritage, one must not be a "real" Mexican. And yet, slavery and slaves were a significant part of Mexico's

colonial experience, and Mexican blacks are still very evidently participating in Mexican life (even though many of their fellow Mexicans often display old racist attitudes that blind them to Africanness in their midst).

5. This is, perhaps, one of the most important reasons why a number of African religions have survived and thrived in the Americas (e.g., Lukumí [misleadingly called Santería], Vodoun, etc.). Today, the largest non-Christian religion in the Americas (also in the United States) might be the Lukumí religion. It came with the Yoruba slaves, and on this side of the Atlantic streamlined itself and grew into an impressive network of communities. The Lukumí religion (known under that name, and also as *Regla de Ocha,* in Cuba and other countries) is known in Brazil as Candomblé.

6. A quote from the nineteenth-century Cuban historian José Antonio Saco. Such "whitening" policies were in place, often by official government decision, in many Latin American countries (e.g., Argentina, Uruguay, Chile, Brazil, Costa Rica, Mexico, etc.). Mexico's Porfirio Díaz encouraged "whitening" immigration policies (e.g., in his attempts to attract French immigrants to Mexico, apparently disregarding and forgiving what the French tried to do to Mexico some years before Díaz's presidency). In Cuba, to pick one of the worst examples, after the end of slavery in the late nineteenth century, the colonial Spanish government implemented an immigration policy with the publicly stated intention of "whitening" the island's population. From 1898 to 1902, the American occupation forces imposed newer immigration laws in order to accelerate the whitening of Cuba. With this policy of the occupiers came other racist attitudes and laws that prior to this time had only rarely been a part of Cuban racial relations. After 1902, the year of Cuban national independence, the consecutive governments of T. Estrada Palma, J. M. Gómez, M. García Menocal, and A. Zayas continued the official immigration policies that were inherited from the colonial and occupation governments and explicitly designed to whiten the country's population. Racial tensions in Cuba during the first decades of the twentieth century boiled over more than once, with disastrous results for all but especially for the population of African descent. The Cuban governments that followed 1933 were either uninterested in immigration policy or quietly racist, and so the immigration laws that favored Europeans remained on the books. Unfortunately, the population of African descent seems to have given up its struggle against these racist policies. The revolutionary government established in 1959, although claiming to have abolished all racist laws, has in fact continued many of the policies of marginalization of Cubans of African descent, and prohibited all expressions of dissatisfaction by nonwhites. Indeed, after nearly

half a century in power, the revolutionary government's top policy-making positions are still held (and have been held) by white *criollos/as*.

7. See chap. 3 in the present volume.

8. Especially the popular music of the Spanish-speaking Caribbean basin, which in turn became the popular rhythms of U.S. Puerto Ricans, Dominican Americans, Cuban Americans, and others. Lukumí sacred music, however, has been sufficiently transformed (as it passed into the popular, nonreligious realm), and so no profanation of the sacred is intended or implied in *rumba, guaguancó, guaracha,* or *salsa* (to name but a few of the popular rhythms). Parallel developments have occurred in other Latin American and U.S. Latino/a cultural contexts.

9. Walter Mercado (a flamboyant Puerto Rican "spiritual star," who combines astrology, Lukumí, and Vodoun, spiritualism, and all sorts of other "spiritual" components in his immensely popular TV and radio programs) is a case in point. He has become a household name among very many U.S. Latinos/as.

5

From Medellín to Santo Domingo

The Unfinished Reflection on Popular Catholicism

Anyone familiar with Latin American Catholicism (and with the Catholicism of U.S. Latinas/os) knows that popular Catholicism is an omnipresent reality. Although not exclusive to Latin American or Latina/o Catholics, popular Catholicism is an identifiable benchmark of Catholic faith.[1]

This article addresses a religious universe that has been called popular religion, popular religiosity, and popular piety, usually interchangeably. It was discussed in three important Latin American episcopal texts: the *Medellín Conclusions* (1968), the *Puebla Document* (1979), and the *Santo Domingo Conclusions* (1992). Puebla also called it, more accurately, popular Catholicism.[2]

The issue of popular religion (popular religiosity, popular piety) is of extreme importance for Latin American and Latina/o Catholicism because—and it is no exaggeration to say—the ordinary way in which Latin American and Latina/o Catholics are Catholic is the way the documents call popular religion, popular religiosity, and popular piety. Hence, this is the real faith of real Catholics.[3] But the issue of popular religion (popular religiosity, popular piety)

The present text was requested by the Catholic theological faculty of J. W. Goethe Universität (Frankfurt, Germany) on the occasion of the fortieth anniversary of the Medellín conference (1968). Consequently, the focus and emphasis of this text are on Latin American Catholicism, although, given the impact of Medellín and Puebla on Latino/a Catholics, much is applicable, *mutatis mutandi*, to U.S. Latina/o Catholicism.

is even more crucial when reflected upon doctrinally and dogmatically.

Latin American Catholics are nearly half of all Catholics in the world; Latinas/os are nearly half of the U.S. Catholic population, and when their numbers are added to Catholics among other populations of Latin American origins in the European Union, they form the overwhelming majority of all Catholics on earth. It can be reasonably concluded that the popular religion (popular religiosity, popular piety) of these Catholics constitutes actual, real-life Catholicism and the real faith of the majority of the people of God. The theological, doctrinal, dogmatic implications of this fact are potentially enormous.

There was insufficient theological reflection on popular Catholicism in the episcopal texts of Medellín, Puebla, and Santo Domingo. Most Latin American bishops, theologians and pastoral agents (in the days after the Second Vatican Council and through the mid-1980s), understandably and justifiably emphasized the social, economic and political reality, and the transformation of Latin America. The final texts of the three episcopal gatherings collectively disregard popular Catholicism, in particular, and popular religion, in general, as a worthy and urgent theological topic, relegating it instead to the "merely" pastoral (if such a category could ever exist) or to the heap of historical vestiges to be superseded in a new Latin America.

In other words, the real faith of real Catholics was not considered sufficiently important to merit sustained theological reflection and renewed pastoral understanding. The result, I believe, was an increasing de facto distance between popular religion (popular religiosity, popular piety), on the one hand, and Latin American theology and ecclesial pastoral care, on the other.[4] By the late 1980s and thereafter, this distance (further instrumentalized by internal ecclesiastical politics) became a de facto separation despite church statements assuring that a divorce was not forthcoming. I would not be surprised if under the current banner of the "new evangelization," we might not be gathering all sorts of agendas and perspectives that are possible only as a consequence of the aforementioned de facto separation.

By insufficiently acknowledging and reflecting theologically on popular religion (popular religiosity, popular piety) as the real-life religion of most ordinary Catholics, the bishops at Medellín, Puebla, and Santo Domingo unfortunately opened the first crack in the de facto separation between the pastoral care of the faith of the people and theological reflection on the people whose faith is undoubtedly popular religion (popular religiosity, popular piety).

The *Medellín Conclusions*, as well as the later *Puebla Document* and *Santo Domingo Conclusions*, use the expressions "popular religion," "popular religiosity," and "popular piety" interchangeably. This common usage, combined with the mediocre quality of these episcopal documents' *theological* reflections on the realities and meanings claimed for the three expressions and the theological and cultural assumptions that lie beneath those reflections, adds up to an unfinished task. Medellín calls for the study of popular religiosity; Puebla teaches the importance of and the respect due to popular piety and popular religion; and Santo Domingo proposes to evangelize popular religion anew, but the three documents' lack of precision, and indeed, their lack of theological depth and rigor, compromises the very possibility of achieving what they request or propose.

In this article, then, I will start by synthetically presenting two quick overviews: the first will consider if and how the spirit of Medellín was carried on by Puebla, Santo Domingo, and the Synod of America; and then a second quick overview will summarize the main teachings on popular religion (popular religiosity, popular piety) proposed by the three episcopal texts. After these two synthetic sections, we will then consider some issues regarding the terminological use of the expressions "popular religion," "popular religiosity," and "popular piety," and find in Puebla's fourth expression, "popular Catholicism," a more adequate and accurate category. Finally I will address the Medellín proposal for the theological study of popular religiosity, suggesting that it still remains an unfinished task after so many decades.

I do not and will not hide from the reader my support for and commitment to the spirit and letter of Medellín, even today, as well as my willing acceptance of the Puebla and Santo Domingo documents as receptions, confirmations, and specifications of the genius of Medellín. The limitations that I find in these three episcopal texts in no way reduce my support for the ecclesial and social transformations first courageously proposed for Latin America by the Second General Conference of the Latin American Episcopate at Medellín in 1968. Therefore, it is in the context of my explicit support for the teaching of these three episcopal conferences that the reader should consider the present article. The reader should be also aware that in the present article I will only be examining the official final texts from Medellín, Puebla, and Santo Domingo.[5]

From the *Medellín Conclusions* to *Ecclesia in America:* A Quick Trajectory of the Spirit of Medellín

No student of Latin American church history can doubt the extraordinary importance and impact of the Second General Conference of that continent's Catholic bishops.[6] Commonly referred to as the Medellín Conference—or simply Medellín—for the Colombian city where it was held in 1968, this episcopal gathering transformed much of the face and commitments of the Catholic Church in Latin America, at least until the middle of John Paul II's pontificate. And even when today many might reasonably argue that the letter and spirit of the *Medellín Conclusions* (as the final text of this conference is called) have been aborted by the church, Medellín's influence has endured in spite of all attempts to derail its influence and magisterial authority.

The fact that Medellín was followed in 1979 by the Third General Conference of Latin American bishops in Puebla, Mexico, is not an irrelevant historical detail. When the Puebla conference convened, attempts were already underway to use the new episcopal gathering to suppress or water down the Medellín impetus in the Latin American church. But the bishops at Puebla kept the flame of Medellín alive; there was no suppression or adulteration of the spirit and letter of the *Medellín Conclusions*. In fact, in some areas, the *Puebla Document*, as this conference's final text is called, furthers and deepens the *Medellín Conclusions*. Had it not been for Puebla's evident and explicit reception of Medellín, the latter's importance and impact might have been lost or permanently adulterated.

Medellín and Puebla were followed in 1992 by the Fourth General Conference, in Santo Domingo, Dominican Republic, but this gathering has been accused of not displaying the same courage, creativity, and spirit as its predecessors. Perhaps. But no one can argue beyond all doubt that there was a backward movement in Santo Domingo. This conference's *Conclusions*, as its final text is called, does not seem to have moved the Latin American ecclesial agenda and commitments forward as much as the earlier two, but there was no backsliding either. Santo Domingo elicited little enthusiasm among Latin American Catholics, and yet a detailed reading of its *Conclusions* would show that, with considerably less enthusiasm than Medellín and Puebla, Santo Domingo did keep alive the Latin American bishops' fundamental commitment to justice, human promotion, and renewed pastoral care. For example, the call for a "new evangelization" in the *Santo Domingo Conclusions* fundamentally repeats what had already been said by Medellín, Puebla, and by Paul VI's *Evangelii Nuntiandi*. On the other hand, Santo Domingo addressed some key issues that had been ignored by, and in some cases deleted from, the *Medellín Conclusions* and the *Puebla Document*. An important example of this are the explicit references to Afro-Latin Americans, their reality, their social and pastoral needs, etc.; Medellín and Puebla had not acknowledged and reflected on one-third of Latin America's population! But in spite of this positive movement, it could be said that, overall, the Santo Domingo conference did little new to promote the spirit of Medellín.

John Paul II's exhortation *Ecclesia in America* (1999), which was the only official document to be published as a result of the Synod of America (held in Rome, 1997), in some ways could be considered a successor to Medellín, Puebla, and Santo Domingo, but in other ways it was not, because the Synod of America included Canadian and United States bishops and, therefore, its character and thematic were not exclusively Latin American. Moreover, because *Ecclesia in America* is an explicitly papal document (in no way claiming episcopal authorship) it is not in the same category as the Medellín, Puebla, and Santo Domingo final texts, which actually reflect the conversations, tensions, and conclusions of the gathered bishops. In some ways *Ecclesia in America* follows the Latin American bishops' three earlier documents, especially the *Santo Domingo Conclusions*, but it adds little to them. The Synod of America, like the Santo Domingo conference, elicited little or no enthusiasm or response from Latin American Catholics and was wholly ignored by Catholics in the United States and Canada. The synod did try (unsuccessfully, in my view) to promote the idea that the churches of Latin American, Canada, and the United States belong together and are responsible for one another. *Ecclesia in America*, as the papal text that followed the synod, does little more to promote this sound idea than state it, and it contributes very little new to what Medellín, Puebla, and Santo Domingo had already taught. Consequently, in this article I will not refer again to *Ecclesia in America*.

From Medellín to Santo Domingo: A Quick Overview of the Teaching on Popular Catholicism in the Three Documents

Before offering this second overview, on the specific teachings on popular Catholicism (popular religion, popular religiosity, popular piety), let me address the evidently awkward issue of terminology.

I have so far used the expressions popular religion, popular religiosity, and popular piety, always jointly, to refer to the faith of ordinary people. In fact, the *Medellín Conclusions*, as well as the *Puebla Document* and the *Santo Domingo Conclusions*, use the three expressions interchangeably, assuming the same basic meaning in the three. But these phrases, in my theological understanding, do not mean the same thing; and it is precisely in the common (and naïvely imprecise) and interchangeable usage of these expressions as equivalent in the three texts that theological difficulties arise.

Later in this article I will explicitly address each of the three expressions, along with the fourth one added by Puebla, popular Catholicism, and some of the difficulties that their interchangeable use as equivalents brings up. For now, let the reader allow me to use the single expression *popular Catholicism* as sufficient, although we will see that it is not used without qualification. There are two reasons for asking to be allowed its use for now: to avoid the stylistic awkwardness of the constant and joint reference to the three (or four) other expressions, and to familiarize the reader with what I believe is the best expression for the conferences' teaching on the Catholic faith of ordinary Catholic people.

What did the bishops gathered at Medellín, Puebla, and Santo Domingo teach about popular Catholicism? There undoubtedly were changes on this topic from 1968 (Medellín) to 1992 (Santo Domingo). One would expect that Santo Domingo would unfold as the end of a progression of the three texts on questions regarding popular Catholicism. In fact, the *Puebla Document* (1979) is the height of the *pastoral* reflection on the topic—a height not built upon by the *Santo Domingo Conclusions*, which also avoids the theological reflection called for by the *Medellín Conclusions*.

Origin of Popular Catholicism

Only the *Santo Domingo Conclusions* directly addresses the question of the origins of Latin American popular Catholicism, although both Puebla and Medellín tangentially *suggest* the origins to be varied, complex, and ultimately explainable interculturally.

The *Santo Domingo Conclusions* (n. 247) explains the origin and existence of popular Catholicism among Latin Americans by appealing exclusively to racial *mestizaje*. There are plenty of cases to confirm *mestizaje* as a partial originating context of Latin American popular Catholicism, but originating context is *not* the same as cause or origin, which is what Santo Domingo suggests by its exclusive use of *mestizaje* to explain the cause and origins of popular Catholicism in Latin America.

Even though Santo Domingo clearly notes that popular Catholicism is an inculturated form of Catholicism, its own explanation (i.e., *mestizaje*) of the genesis of the popular religious universe ignores the fact that many Latin American forms of popular Catholicism were imported from Spain and Portugal and were not created as a response to racial mixture in the Americas. The text further ignores the fact that popular Catholicism is also present among Latin American groups with no history of racial *mestizaje*. In other words, the facts of popular Catholicism demonstrate that *mestizaje* is not the sole explanation for the existence or origin of popular Catholicism in Latin America (and arguably not the best explanation either) but only one of the contextual elements to be taken into consideration. Although Santo Domingo claims to be only repeating the *Puebla Document*'s teaching on the matter (referring to Puebla, n. 307), the latter document in fact does not propose *mestizaje* as the cause or genesis of popular Catholicism.

Definition(s) of Popular Catholicism

If we go beyond the question of origins (wisely sidestepped and only tangentially touched by Medellín and Puebla), we enter richer territory. We see that the three documents offer their respective summary definitions of popular Catholicism, and here it is that we find the interchangeable and imprecise use of the expressions popular religion, popular religiosity, and popular piety (Puebla alone adding a fourth expression, popular Catholicism).

The *Puebla Document* explicitly equates the expressions, jointly defining them as "a complex of profound beliefs, sealed by God, and of basic attitudes derived from those convictions, as well as the expressions that manifest them. It is the form or cultural existence that religion adopts among a specific people. The religion of the Latin American people, in its most characteristic cultural form, is an expression of the Catholic faith. It is a popular Catholicism" (n. 444). Inadvertently perhaps, the *Puebla Document* thereby adds the fourth expression to discuss the popular religious universe: popular Catholicism—still interchangeable with the other three expressions, but a more accurate term to describe the popular religious universe.

Even though Puebla confuses the terminology, it remains the episcopal text that most closely examines Latin American popular Catholicism, especially from a *pastoral* perspective. Compared to Medellín's limited references to popular Catholicism, Puebla is a more thorough reflection. Compared to Santo Domingo, Puebla is creative, forward looking, and more pastorally aware.

Regardless of the reference to *mestizaje* mentioned above, the *Santo Domingo Conclusions* adds nothing significant or new to Medellín's and Puebla's understanding of popular Catholicism. Its references to it are in nn. 18, 36, 38-39, and 255. Santo Domingo defines "popular religiosity (as) a privileged expression of the inculturation of the faith. It involves not only religious expressions or forms but also a wide number of values, criteria, behaviors and attitudes, born of Catholic dogma, that constitute Latin America's 'popular wisdom' and cultural matrix" (n. 36). Indeed, there is nothing beyond Puebla here, and considerably less.

What does Medellín understand as popular religiosity (its preferred term)? In 6.2-6 and 6.10 (but especially in 6.2), the *Medellín Conclusions* sees popular Catholicism as *a* result of Latin America's earliest evangelization. It describes popular Catholicism as a web of vows and promises, of pilgrimages and devotions, and of culturally expected sacramental practices (for the most part involving and surrounding baptism and first communion). Although popular Catholicism is often deficient in true moral practices and in authentic commitment to the church, it is deemed by Medellín to be a repository of authentic Christian virtues. In the *Medellín Conclusions*, contemporary science is viewed as causing a crisis within popular Catholicism, because the latter has maintained an understanding of God as the direct cause of and answer to all human and natural events and questions and is contradicted by science's more modern perspectives.[7] Medellín laid down a descriptively synthetic view of popular Catholicism that was later taken up and developed by Puebla.

Approaches to Popular Religion

In their respective pastoral approaches and responses to popular Catholicism, all three documents are in close agreement, although Medellín must be credited with first proposing the respectful perspective toward the Catholic peoples' religion that will later reappear in Puebla and Santo Domingo. Indeed, it was Medellín, and only Medellín, that explicitly requested the systematic theological study of popular Catholicism.

The *Medellín Conclusions* (especially n. 6.4) very wisely teaches that popular Catholicism must not be judged or evaluated with the same interpretive tools designed for and used on Western religious practices. Because popular Catholicism is mostly, although not exclusively, a religious universe created by and among the poor (in both rural and urban contexts), it should not be examined in the same manner and with the same criteria as the religious universe of the middle and upper classes of society.

The expressions of popular Catholicism might be deemed deformed, or mixed with ancestral religious practices and beliefs, or subject to the tyranny of superstition and magic; but in spite of its apparent limitations, popular Catholicism can legitimately be interpreted as the culturally authentic religious practices and beliefs of Catholics that, in limited but authentic ways, attempt to convey and express Christian truth.

Because of this authenticity (n. 8.2), popular Catholicism must not be disregarded, undervalued, or ignored (theologically or pastorally) because it can be a point of departure for a more comprehensive evangelization. More especially, it should be systematically studied by theology and the social sciences. Popular Catholicism's cultural and ecclesial role and doctrinal contents are also in need of this scientific study. In n. 6.10, Medellín insists that theologians and social scientists take popular Catholicism seriously as an object of study, and that they systematically research its expressions, contents, and roles. Several decades after Medellín, we see that its call to theologians has not been sufficiently heeded, because popular Catholicism seems to have attracted the attention only of pastoral agents and social scientists while remaining outside the research interests of the theological community in Latin America and elsewhere (although, of course, there have been some exceptions).

In the eleven years that passed between Medellín and Puebla a pastoral consensus grew in Latin America that viewed popular Catholicism more positively, but (what is more worrisome), it has been viewed as an almost exclusively *pastoral* issue.

The *Puebla Document* takes the episcopal *pastoral* reflection furthest, especially in nn. 444-69, and also in nn. 6, 234, 343, 368, 910-15, 936-37, and 959-61. But the apparent consensus in Puebla regarding popular Catholicism did not include or even acknowledge Medellín's explicit call for theology's systematic and scientific study of this popular religion. Puebla takes the *pastoral* reflection to new heights, but not the *theological* one. This task remained undone, within the Puebla document as well as within the effervescent Latin American theological community.[8]

Puebla's understanding or definition of popular Catholicism receives and repeats Medellín's, adding some new terms, but with greater sophistication and breadth (e.g., nn. 444-57). Compared with Medellín's intuitions or perspective on the importance and meaning of popular Catholicism, there are really few new intuitions or perspectives in Puebla. But the *Puebla Document* does expand beyond Medellín's teaching by an emphatic, well-argued, and *pastorally* sophisticated request that popular Catholicism be taken seriously by pastoral agents, and that it be pastorally "accompanied" and "discerned" throughout Latin America. Medellín had said this much, but there it had not appeared as emphatically and pervasively as it did in the *Puebla Document*.

Puebla was deeply concerned with the consequences of rapid urbanization on popular Catholicism (e.g., nn. 460 and 466), and thus it directs many of its pastoral recommendations to adapting, discerning, and evaluating popular Catholicism in order for it to remain a vital religious force in urbanized Latin America with its increasingly secularized mentality. Medellín was more modest than Puebla in its specific pastoral proposals and reflections on popular Catholicism, but in the long term it was immensely wiser and potentially more revolutionary when it requested the scientific, theological study of popular Catholicism.

The approach of the *Santo Domingo Conclusions* to popular Catholicism is also pastoral. It receives and repeats Puebla in this regard, but again sidesteps Medellín's call for the scientific, theological study of popular religion. Santo Domingo's references to it are in nn. 18, 36, 38-39, and 255. Nowhere does it deviate from Puebla's intuitions or perspectives, although Santo Domingo's reflections on the topic are generally less sophisticated, less pastorally aware, and less comprehensive. Maybe the bishops assumed a widespread knowledge and acceptance of the Puebla recommendations, or maybe they preferred to simply refer to Puebla (as they occasionally did in reference to popular Catholicism); but whatever their reasoning might have been, and especially given Santo Domingo's focus on a new evangelization, it strikes me as unfortunate that their *Conclusions* did not expand or deepen Puebla's pastoral intuitions, reflections, and recommendations on popular Catholicism. It was indeed a gain that Santo Domingo did not backtrack on this issue, but it offers precious little that is new.

Medellín's call for the theological, scientific study of popular Catholicism is nowhere to be found in the *Santo Domingo Conclusions*—it does seem that the Puebla consensus (i.e., that popular Catholicism is mainly, if not exclusively, a *pastoral* concern) was also received and repeated by Santo Domingo.

Behind the Terminology

It is time to consider the issue of terminology raised by Medellín's, Puebla's, and Santo Domingo's use of the expressions "popular religion," "popular religiosity," and "popular piety"—and, because of Puebla, also "popular Catholicism"—as interchangeable and equivalent.

The reader will recall that I had earlier requested permission to generally use *popular Catholicism* in the present article, promising to later justify this use. Let me now do what I had promised.

The three documents we are studying use the terms "popular religion," "popular religiosity," and "popular piety" to mean precisely what Puebla explicitly calls "popular Catholicism" (n. 444). In other words, the expressions are seen to be interchangeable and equivalent in meaning because they all refer to a style of Catholicism created by and among the poor of Latin America since the days of the first evangelization as their authentic cultural expression of Catholic Christianity. That is the reason why the three documents do not hesitate to say that popular religion, popular religiosity, and popular piety are a legitimate and authentic inculturation of the Catholic faith in Latin America; they are popular Catholicism. This interpretation is often repeated in the three documents. But we may wonder if those three expressions are indeed equal to and coextensive with popular Catholicism.[9]

Religiosity

Catholicism in its "popular" Latin American inculturation (with its pluses and its minuses) is certainly a religion; it can justifiably be called popular Catholicism and even a popular religion. But "religiosity"? The meaning of *religiosidad* in Spanish (or *religiosidade* in Portuguese) does not equate it with "religion," and therefore it cannot be naïvely used as interchangeable or equivalent to it. "Religiosity" implies and carries a dismissive tone, and is not "as good" as a "religion"; it is almost a "pseudo" religion, appearing to be but not actually being the equivalent of "religion."

Is this what the three documents understand by popular Catholicism? In some places they seem to imply as much, but their shared respect for and defense of the Christian authenticity of popular Catholicism as inculturated *Catholic* faith make us wonder. Could the bishops, wishing to promote the care of and respect for popular religion, really intend to define it in such dismissive terms?

It is more likely that "religiosity" was chosen by Medellín, because there was no other term in use in the 1960s for the popular religious universe. We must recall that Medellín wisely and modestly admitted, expected, and required the social-scientific and systematic theological study of the popular religious universe; the *Medellín Conclusions* uses the term "religiosity" without in any way equating its then-current usage with what it suspected might be involved in the complex popular religious universe (and thus asked to have this universe scientifically examined). Puebla and Santo Domingo, however, because of their unexplained assumption that popular Catholicism was mostly if not exclusively a *pastoral* concern, placed their reflections and recommendations squarely within the pastoral sphere and for the most part ignored explicitly theological questions on the issue. Had there been alternative terminologies in the 1960s as well as widespread, sustained, scientific and systematic theological research into popular Catholicism, Medellín (and later Puebla and Santo Domingo) would not have used the category "religiosity." Its use objectively contradicts the documents' generally respectful and accepting interpretations of popular Catholicism.

Piety

The reference to popular piety is somewhat different. There is no dismissive tone in "piety," but its common usage in Spanish and

Portuguese (especially in the 1970s, the decade preceding Puebla) referred almost exclusively to Catholic prayer life and its multiple practices, which were often associated with what at the time were called "para-liturgies." The pious person was the prayerful person. And so popular piety was mainly the prayer practices of the people; included in these were individual as well as communal practices, such as pilgrimages and many other pious expressions of the people. It is evident that the Catholicism of the people includes popular piety, and so the term adequately refers to much within popular Catholicism, but it is not coextensive with it. Within popular Catholicism there are beliefs, ethical expectations, etc., that cannot be simplistically explained as no more than the pious, prayerful practices of the people. "Popular piety," consequently, is an adequate term to employ (as Puebla and Santo Domingo do) but only if its meaning is not equated with "popular Catholicism," and if it is understood to be only a part of it.

Religion

And so, if "religiosity" is inadequate and inaccurate, and thus unacceptable, and if "piety" is acceptable but only under the conditions just stated, then what about the expression "popular religion"? It too cannot be equated or used interchangeably with the other expressions, but for other reasons.

Medellín, Puebla, and Santo Domingo, in their respective reflections on the popular religious universe, in fact and undoubtedly referred to popular *Catholicism* and to nothing else. Although occasionally acknowledging the influence of non-Christian religions on popular Catholicism, the three documents agree on their identification and defense of popular Catholicism as Catholicism. There is no question on this. It might be Catholicism in need of discernment, purification, better instruction, and even of a new evangelization, but it is nevertheless the authentically inculturated *Catholic* faith. There is no question on this point in the three documents. But if we pay some attention to the general expression "popular religion," we note that it is not and cannot be equated, at least in Latin America, with popular Catholicism or used interchangeably with it.

"Popular religion" means that the religious universe referred to is indeed a "religion," and that it exists and perhaps was created by and among ordinary people, most probably the poor. There is nothing in the expression "popular religion" to suggest a dismissive tone or to allow it to be reduced to only prayerful practices (although any religion will of necessity include these). More to our point, there is nothing in the expression "popular religion" to require its identification, and therefore, its equation and interchangeability, with Catholicism. Popular Catholicism is certainly a popular religion, but not all popular religion is Catholic. That is the first point to make on this issue.

The use of "popular religion" and "popular Catholicism" as interchangeable and equivalent is neither adequate nor acceptable, unless we first explicitly limit to popular Catholicism the religion we are referring to. But none of the three documents does this, and thus the assumption that popular religion (concretely in Puebla and Santo Domingo) is equal to popular Catholicism is unfortunate and mistaken.

The second point to make on this issue is more important. In Latin America there have always existed non-Christians and non-Christian religions among the poor. To assume, as the three documents do, that all popular religion is Catholic in Latin America is simply untenable. Medellín, Puebla, and Santo Domingo themselves explicitly recognize the existence of other religious universes in Latin America—from separated Christians, to "oriental religions," to Judaism, to surviving indigenous religions, to African religions.

It is unfortunate that the three Latin American episcopal texts speak of non-Christian religions generally as either newcomers to the continent, and thus foreign to the real roots and meaning of *latinoamericanidad*,[10] or as vestiges of the colonial and even precolonial past. These non-Christian religions are either doomed to disappear in time or, at best, are in need of profound purification and, as a consequence, are of little use to the future of *latino-americanidad.* In other words, Medellín, Puebla, and Santo Domingo, when speaking of non-Christian religions, do not take their *latinoamericanidad* seriously and do not even perceive their profound and multisecular presence among millions of Latin Americans. When we read the three texts, we get the impression that the bishops very much wanted to equate *latinoamericanidad* with Catholicism, to the exclusion or diminution of every other religious universe.

The African religions of Latin America are a very clear example (together with the native religions) of the difficulties created by the confused terminology in the three documents.[11]

It is difficult to understand why the *Medellín Conclusions* said nothing, directly or tangentially, about the millions of Latin Americans who trace their ancestry to Africa and to the slavery of Africans in the continent. These Afro-Latin Americans, who constitute one-third of the continent's population, merited not one word from the bishops at Medellín, in contrast to indigenous, native populations, who are explicitly mentioned. It might be argued that Afro-Latin Americans were implied in all of the *Medellín Conclusions,* but the fact remains that other, much smaller groups were explicitly referred to in the text; and so one must honestly admit that the absence of all reference to Afro-Latin Americans in Medellín might need to be explained as an example of Latin America's ingrained racism in both society and church, as well as by the complete absence of racial analysis in the theology and social sciences of the 1960s.

The *Puebla Document* barely acknowledges the existence of Afro-Latin Americans in passing (nn. 8 [note], 34, 307, 365, 409-10, 415, 441, and 451). Puebla makes no particular pastoral recommendation in reference to them, and it does not reflect on what the contributions or presence of one-third of Latin Americans might mean for the church and the continent. There is but one reference in Puebla (n. 451) to the African religions of Latin America, and it appears unexplainably under the category of a "Catholic popular piety."

It was Santo Domingo, among the three texts, that finally and for the first time paid *some* sustained attention to the African presence in Latin America (nn. 20, 30, 38, 137-38, 243-51, and 299). Admitting the horrors of slavery and the cultural richness brought to the Americas by enslaved Africans and their descendants, Santo Domingo asks their forgiveness for the cowardly silence and complicity of Catholics during the centuries of the slave trade, and for the consequences inflicted on Afro-Latin Americans by racism and bigotry, which were oftentimes condoned by the church. Santo Domingo affirms the church's desire to support Afro-Latin Americans in their struggles for equality, justice, and identity. In nn. 137 and 138 the *Santo Domingo Conclusions* explicitly acknowledge African religions in Latin America, and call for interreligious dialogue with them, *because* these religions are interpreted as *semina Verbi* ("seeds of the Word").

There are, and there have always been, more religions in Latin America than Catholicism. Were we to take seriously the demographics of the Afro-Latin American religions, we would need to contend with almost twenty million Latin Americans who do not look to Catholicism as theirs, but who nevertheless have impacted and have been impacted by it in its *popular* inculturation.

Furthermore, these millions of Latin Americans have been, are, and will be Latin Americans, and thus to assume, as the bishops apparently do, that *latinoamericanidad,* from the viewpoint of religion, is to be understood exclusively or best by Catholicism is offensive to one-third of Latin America. The fact that the institutions of the church were the largest slave owners in Latin America is not an irrelevant or easily forgotten fact, as Santo Domingo itself had to recognize, and thus to claim that *latinoamericanidad* is best understood through the perspective of the largest slave master in Latin America's history is truly, morally, and factually, incomprehensible. Historically, Latin America was as much shaped by European colonialism as it was by African slavery, and in many places by a strong indigenous heritage.

To think of Latin America as, for the most part, religiously monochrome is historical nonsense. Because of this, it smells of neocolonialism to claim, as our three documents do, that Catholicism is *the* religious matrix of Latin America. Catholics cannot historically claim this any more than the millions who participate in native or African religions. The bishops could more modestly and correctly have affirmed that Catholicism has been *one* of the religious matrices of Latin America—a very important matrix, yes, but not the only one.

Furthermore, and more explicitly in reference to my discussion of the expression "popular religion," non-Christian religions in Latin America have had and continue to have what might be called their "authentically inculturated faith" in Latin America—just as Catholicism has. In other words, there is not just *one* popular religion in Latin America that can be equated to popular Catholicism. Other popular religions exist on the continent, Christian and non-Christian, and these are true religions that trace their Latin American form to and among the poor (and this is especially true in the case of the indigenous peoples and of the Afro-Latin Americans).

Therefore, can the term "popular religion" be used for "popular Catholicism"? Yes, but only as long as we clearly understand that popular Catholicism is but *one* of Latin America's several popular religions, and that the two expressions are clearly not interchangeable or equivalent. It is unfortunate that neither Medellín, nor Puebla, nor Santo Domingo employed this terminological precision when discussing popular Catholicism.

Unfinished Business: The Theological Study of Popular Catholicism

I began this article by suggesting that a proposal made by the *Medellín Conclusions* (n. 6.10) has remained an unfinished task, a dream to be realized, and thus it still is unfinished business: the *theological* study of popular Catholicism in Latin America and elsewhere.[12]

Latin America has been blessed by continent-wide episcopal gatherings that have with courage, creativity, and sophistication proposed sound pastoral approaches toward popular Catholicism. But these same conferences have not been as successful in their theological understanding of popular Catholicism and in distinguishing it from other popular religious forms or from other Latin American popular religions. Indeed, these three general conferences of the Latin American episcopate apparently did not see the potentially immense impact of popular Catholicism on dogmatic, theological reflection. Medellín, perhaps, was the only general conference that understood that popular Catholicism could not be limited to exclusively pastoral concerns.

The final documents of the Medellín, Puebla, and Santo Domingo conferences not only display terminological imprecision and confusion, but in fact they misunderstand and at times misrepresent the popular Catholicism they so want to respect and pastorally care for.

The *Medellín Conclusions*, in its modesty on this issue, perhaps gave us the best route to address the concerns raised by popular Catholicism: respectful and creative pastoral care bound to rigorous, scientific theological research. Unfortunately, the ties that bind the two sides of this one route were not recognized by either the *Puebla Document* or the *Santo Domingo Conclusions*.

It can be reasonably argued that neither Puebla nor Santo Domingo (nor Medellín, for that matter) intended to be *theological* gatherings, but rather meetings of bishops; and, consequently, the intent was always and remained explicitly *pastoral*. This is certainly true, but what is definitely not true is the underlying assumption that the bishops of the church could make sound pastoral reflections and recommendations *without* sound theological reflection as well.

Each of the three final documents includes extensive sections on doctrine that the bishops expected to be presented in theologically accurate and dogmatically solid arguments. These *pastoral* documents, therefore, needed and expected *theological* expertise and research for their doctrinal parts.

We may honestly ask, then, Why is there no theological reflection or expertise in the sections dealing explicitly with popular Catholicism? Why is there this absence in the sections dealing with the real, inculturated Catholic faith of real Latin American Catholics? It was the bishops themselves, after all, who correctly labeled popular Catholicism as the "authentically inculturated faith" of Latin American Catholics! The answer possibly lies in the erroneous assumption that the faith of the people is, really, a pastoral and not a theological issue. Doctrinally, this is untenable, of course.

A very important project, proposed by the *Medellín Conclusions*, remains undone: the dogmatic, doctrinal, theological reflection on popular Catholicism. This reflection, I insist, cannot be divorced from pastoral concerns (because these presuppose that reflection, and vice versa), but the reflection is not to be focused on and limited only to pastoral issues. Popular Catholicism is, involves, and provokes dogmatic, doctrinal issues. It is this reflection that has been missing in Latin America and elsewhere.

Many profoundly dogmatic questions arise when we theologically confront popular Catholicism. And many profoundly dogmatic issues are questioned by a theological study of popular Catholicism. For example, Can we speak of the people of God (and, hence, of church) dogmatically, and somehow pretend that the ordinary way in which faithful Catholics are Catholic is doctrinally irrelevant to, for, and in ecclesiology? If real Catholics and their faith are doctrinally irrelevant to ecclesiology, then what church, which people of God, can ecclesiology refer to without falling into fantasy? What impact does the ordinary faith of Catholics have on such theological topics as the *sensus fidelium* and the *sensus fidei*, the reception of doctrines, the infallibility of the church, the necessity of church, the doctrine of revelation, the reality and witness of tradition, the theological meaning of sacrament, and dogmatic issues implied by inculturation and interculturality? And so many more.

Can we theologize on these and other topics without explicit regard and concern for the contents, traditioning, and culturality of the ordinary faith of most ordinary Catholics on earth? Unless theologians choose to justify a sectarian approach to Catholicism, which is ultimately unjustifiable, there is no possibility of theologizing legitimately within and about Catholicism by disregarding the real-life faith of the people of God. In other words, theological, dogmatic, doctrinal systematic research and reflection on popular Catholicism is absolutely indispensable. This is the unfinished task—indeed, in most places, the undone task.

This is not the place to offer all of the arguments in favor of this reflection, and it is not either the place for offering methodological proposals and resources for this task. This has already been done elsewhere.[13]

Limiting myself to the three Latin American episcopal documents, I wonder if we may not honestly ask, Had Medellín's proposed theological reflection been taken seriously, would Santo Domingo's explicit statements about women (nn. 104-10) have been written as they were, and with the content and perspectives they display? Had Medellín's proposed theological reflection been done, would Puebla's and Santo Domingo's so-called doctrinal preambles (e.g., Puebla, nn. 170-303 and 316-39; Santo Domingo, nn. 1-15) have been written as they were or would they have included other issues, grounds, and perspectives? I am not suggesting that Puebla and Santo Domingo were grounded on faulty doctrinal foundations because they missed Medellín's call for doctrinal reflection on popular Catholicism, but I am saying that at least significant sections of those two documents would have been written differently if the bishops and their theological advisers had picked up Medellín's challenge and had actually engaged in systematic doctrinal reflection on popular Catholicism.[14]

My sole interest here is to indicate that the *Medellín Conclusions* made the proposal, but that the *Puebla Document* and the *Santo Domingo Conclusions* missed the point and avoided the task. Unfortunately, Latin American (and other) theologians—with the exceptions noted—have mostly avoided the task too, thereby ignoring the dogmatic issues that popular Catholicism would certainly raise if the real, inculturated faith of the immense majority of Catholics were taken truly seriously as *locus theologicus*. Today's great theological debates revolve around issues pertaining to cultures, ecclesiology, and revelation; and so, how can theologians ignore the fact that the real faith of the immense majority of Catholics is the true and indispensable source of their theologizing on topics where "the people" are the indispensable *locus* and protagonist? Perhaps it is now the time to finally engage Medellín's wise proposal.

Notes

1. This is evident from church history and from more recent ecclesiastical documents (see, e.g., Paul VI's *Evangelii Nuntiandi* and numerous pastoral letters from bishops' conferences throughout the world). For an example of the very early appearance of popular Catholicism in the history of the church, see J. O'Callahan, *El cristianismo popular en el Egipto del siglo II* (Madrid: Ed. Cristiandad, 1979). Social scientists have been studying Latin American popular Catholicism for decades; some of the key contributors appear below, in note 12.

2. The editions of the three documents used for the present article are: *Medellín: Conclusiones,* 6th ed. (Bogotá: Secretariado General del CELAM, 1971); *Documento de Puebla,* first official authorized ed. (Santo Domingo: Conferencia Episcopal Dominicana/Ediciones Amigo del Hogar, 1979); *Conclusiones de la IV Conferencia del Episcopado Latinoamericano,* first official authorized ed. (Santo Domingo: Conferencia Episcopal Dominicana/Ediciones MSC, 1992). See also G. Doig Klinge, *Diccionario Río-Medellín-Puebla-Santo Domingo* (Bogotá: Ediciones San Pablo, 1994).

3. On popular Catholicism's theological importance and role as *locus theologicus*, see O. O. Espín, *The Faith of the People: Theological Reflections on Popular Catholicism* (Maryknoll, N.Y.: Orbis Books, 1997). See also idem, "Explorations in the Theology of Grace and Sin," in *From the Heart of Our People: Latino/a Explorations in Catholic Systematic Theology,* ed. O. O. Espín and M. H. Díaz (Maryknoll, N.Y.: Orbis Books, 1999), and idem, "Grace and Humanness," in *We Are a People! Initiatives in Hispanic American Theology,* ed. R. S. Goizueta (Minneapolis: Fortress Press, 1992).

4. This was already perceived by Chilean theologian S. Galilea, "The Theology of Liberation and the Place of Folk Religion," *Concilium* 136

(1980): 40-45. J. C. Scannone and J. L. Segundo are two Latin American theologians of the same generation with (is it an exaggeration to say?) diametrically opposed evaluations of popular Catholicism; for a comparative study of their conclusions, see M. R. Candelaria, *Popular Religion and Liberation: The Dilemma of Liberation Theology* (Albany: State University of New York Press, 1990).

5. Commentaries on and evaluations of the three conferences, their processes, and their final and allied texts are plentiful and easily accessible. A complete study of the topics raised in this article would require, consequently, a systematic consideration of the final texts coupled with the allied texts (i.e., messages, letters, minutes of meetings, preparatory texts, etc.) and even personal accounts of witnesses. Such a complete study is not possible here, and it is not intended.

6. The First General Conference of the Latin American Episcopate was held in Rio de Janeiro, Brazil, in 1955. Because of the ecclesial renewal brought about by the Second Vatican Council a decade later, most of the Rio conference's pastoral recommendations were set aside by the Latin American bishops themselves, with the explicit agreement of Paul VI, when the Second General Conference was convened at Medellín in 1968. The final document from the First General Conference was officially called the *Rio Conclusions*, thereby setting the precedent for the similar naming of the Medellín and Santo Domingo official final texts. The Puebla final text has been the only one to be called a *Document*.

7. On this point, and on so many others, we cannot forget that Medellín and the other two episcopal gatherings occurred within their own particular cultural, historical, theological (and many other) contexts. This fact requires that we always interpret the texts against the background of the setting that made possible the thought reflected in the respective texts. This limits much of what we wish might have been said but, given the historical and cultural circumstances, was not yet able to be said. With the Second Vatican Council the Medellín Conference shared an interpretation of its modern context that today, perhaps, we would not presuppose or assume.

8. With few exceptions, popular Catholicism is absent from the works of most Latin American theologians. Segundo Galilea and Juan Carlos Scannone are among the few exceptions, as indicated in an earlier note. Indeed, this was the main point of Galilea's article ("The Theology of Liberation and the Place of Folk Religion" [n. 4]). At their theologies' risk, liberation theologians were ignoring the people's actual faith. It does seem odd to me today that liberation theologians' insistent, necessary, and important method-

ological starting point (i.e., the systematic analysis of the actual reality of the people) could have been so disregarded and sidestepped by them whenever the analysis of the *popular* religious component of the people's actual reality was methodologically required. In the few instances when they eventually addressed popular Catholicism, liberation theologians inadvertently chose *their own* descriptions and interpretations of the people's popular religious universe instead of the *people's* descriptions and interpretations, thereby voiding and avoiding the systematic theological study of the religious component of reality as the people's reality, and consequently placing at risk the basic methodological premise of liberation theology. Many of us are familiar with and supportive of liberation theology's emphatic option for the poor. But has the analysis of the poor's *reality* not been the *poor's*? In other words, *whose* analysis of the poor's reality is it or should it be? These questions should be methodologically raised in reference to the analysis by liberation theologians of popular Catholicism and of social reality as interpreted by the poor (or I should say, in reference to the lack of such analysis). Liberation theologians were supposed to analyze and interpret the reality of the poor as the theologians methodologically saw necessary. This I do not question; but what I do wonder about is the consistency of application of a methodological starting point (very explicitly and insistently claimed by liberation theologians) that said that theology had to take seriously the analysis of the poor's reality as methodologically first, and then proceeded to void and ignore the poor's own analysis and interpretation of their own reality. This is particularly true, given that the Latin American poor's analysis and interpretation of their own reality has been, is, and for the foreseeable future will continue to be explicitly constructed and expressed through the hermeneutic, interpretive categories of popular Catholicism (i.e., the people's authentic and legitimate inculturation of the faith).

9. It might be useful to refer the reader to several of my studies that address and develop the arguments about the use and meaning of the four expressions used by Medellín, Puebla, and Santo Domingo. See "Popular Catholicism among Latinos," in *Hispanic Catholic Culture in the U.S.,* ed. J. Dolan and A. F. Deck (Notre Dame, Ind.: University of Notre Dame Press, 1994); "Religiosidad popular. Un aporte para su definición y hermenéutica," *Estudios Sociales* 58 (1984): 41-57; "Popular Catholicism: Alienation or Hope?" in *Aliens in Jerusalem,* ed. F. F. Segovia and A. M. Isasi-Díaz (Minneapolis: Fortress Press, 1995); "Popular Religion as Epistemology (of Suffering)," in *Journal of Hispanic/Latino Theology* 2 (1994): 55-78; and *The Faith of the People* (n. 3, above).

10. *Latinoamericanidad* is a term that refers to the quality of "Latin American-ness" of something or someone.

11. On the importance and theological analysis of Afro-Latin American religions, see my *Evangelización y religiones negras,* vols. I-IV (Rio de Janeiro: Ed. da PUC, 1984), and more recently my paper "Toward a Latino/a Theology of Religions: In Dialogue with the Lukumí Religion" presented at the 2004 convention of the Catholic Theological Society of America, in Reston, Virginia. This paper appears as chapter 3 in the present volume.

12. U.S. Latino/a Catholic theologians are perhaps, as a body (usually gathered around the Academy of Catholic Hispanic Theologians of the U.S.), the group that has more consistently and over two decades systematically reflected on popular Catholicism as *locus theologicus.* Important in this regard, and from different methodological perspectives, are the works of Miguel Díaz, Roberto Goizueta, Jeannette Rodríguez, Ada M. Isasi-Díaz, Alejandro García-Rivera, Jean-Pierre Ruiz, Nancy Pineda-Madrid, María Pilar Aquino, Michelle González, and my own work. In Latin America, Diego Irarrázaval, Segundo Galilea, Ivonne Gebara, and Juan Carlos Scannone are primary examples. Latin American social scientists are important too in this regard, especially Carlos Steil, Pedro Ribeiro de Oliveira, Renato Ortiz, Carlos da Matta, Christián Parker, Otto Maduro, and the scholars gathered in the Asociación de Cientistas Sociales en el MERCOSUR.

13. See, for example, my *The Faith of the People* (n. 3, above), as well as R. S. Goizueta, *Caminemos con Jesús: Toward a Hispanic/Latino Theology of Accompaniment* (Maryknoll, N.Y.: Orbis Books, 1995); M. H. Díaz, *On Being Human: Hispanic and Rahnerian Perspectives* (Maryknoll, N.Y.: Orbis Books, 2002); and M. P. Aquino, "Theological Method in U.S. Latino/a Theology," in *From the Heart of Our People* (n. 3, above).

14. I should again remind the reader that the Puebla bishops and their theological advisers reflected the consensus that seems to have developed after Medellín (but not as a necessary consequence thereof) that regarded popular Catholicism as mostly a pastoral issue.

Also of interest

The Faith of the People
Theological Reflections on Popular Catholicism
Orlando O. Espín
ISBN 1-57075-111-0

"A truly original, creative, critical breakthrough in the appreciation of the *sensus fidelium* of the poor as the indispensable starting point of theological reflection."
—*Virgil Elizondo*

From the Heart of Our People
Latino/a Explorations in Catholic Systematic Theology
Orlando O. Espín and Miguel H. Díaz, editors

"Ca